SWEETNESS FOLLOWS

THE STORY OF SAM AND THE TREAT OF THE WEEK

KATY HOUSTON

May sweetness follow you,
Katy

Sweetness Follows

THE STORY OF SAM AND THE TREAT OF THE WEEK

Copyright © 2012 by
Katy's Kitchen, LLC
Katy S. Houston
106 Rockingham Circle
Ridgeland, Mississippi 39157
601-790-4488

Food and Chapter Opener Photography © by Greg Campbell
Food Stylist: Patty Roper
The title of this book, "Sweetness Follows," used with permission of R.E.M (page 13).

Produced and Manufactured by
Favorite Recipes® Press
An imprint of
SOUTHWESTERN Publishing Group

P.O. Box 305142
Nashville Tennessee 37230
1-800-358-0560

Project Editor: Tanis Westbrook
Art Director: Steve Newman
Book Design: Sheri Ferguson

Library of Congress Control Number: 2012939748
ISBN: 978-0-615-58339-6

All rights reserved. No part of this publication may be reproduced in any form or by any means, electronic or mechanical, including photocopying and recording, or by any information storage and retrieval systems, without prior written permission from Katy's Kitchen, LLC.

Manufactured in the United States of America
First Printing: 2012
5,000 copies

Sweetness Follows

THE STORY OF SAM AND THE TREAT OF THE WEEK

KATY HOUSTON

preface

This book is a collection of recipes for desserts that were made on a weekly basis for a very special young man, Sam Lane.

As our children grow up, some are fortunate enough to have a best friend along the way. They share so many experiences (some good, some not-so-good) and milestones over the years that this friend eventually seems like a part of your own family. For our son Andrew, Sam has been that friend. That is why, when Sam suffered a life-changing accident, our family was so affected. With a long and uncertain road of recovery ahead of him, I was at a loss of what I could do. Doing nothing was not an option. I decided I would cook, and that is what I did! Every week I took Sam a different dessert. Standing on his doorstep every Monday morning was my unspoken way of saying, "I am with you in this, and I care about you." In my mind I was saying, "If this brings you one ounce of happiness today, I will have done what I tried to do." I would leave every week looking forward to what I would cook next. In this book you will find the recipes for these desserts, and you will also see how his strong and loyal family, loved by so many, have found their own ways of giving back to others in return.

In the South, friends, family, and food are all tied together. This story about Sam celebrates all three.

—Katy Houston

"From preschool on, Andrew and I always stuck together. That took us to the University of Georgia in Athens, where we shared a house on Hancock Avenue. On a Friday afternoon in the spring of our junior year, I was riding my bike along Prince Street in Athens with a group in an organized ride to raise bicycle awareness. During the ride, I was hit by a drunk driver and sustained a traumatic brain injury. My life was put in jeopardy. Fortunately, Athens Regional Medical Center was just down the road and I could receive the initial care I needed there. I remained in a coma for five weeks, during which time I was flown by air ambulance to St. Dominic's Hospital in Jackson, Mississippi. This was followed by a two-month stay at Mississippi Methodist Rehabilitation Center (MMRC), where I received intensive physical, occupational, and speech therapy.

While I was in MMRC, Mrs. Houston visited often. When I was able to eat again, she told me she was going to "feed me back to health." Every Monday morning for 62 consecutive weeks, she brought a different homemade dessert to my front door. It reminded me of the treats that I had enjoyed often in the kitchen at Andrew's house. Naturally, the consistent weekly confection became known as the "Treat of the Week." Even if she was going to be out of town, she arranged for someone to deliver an ice cream dessert she had prepared before leaving. These continued until I moved to Oxford to resume my university studies at Ole Miss.

I hope you enjoy these recipes as much as I did and remember how much a little sweetness adds to life."

—Sam Lane

foreword

I first knew Katy Houston when we were both little girls and she would come to visit her grandmother in the summers in Rosedale, a small Mississippi delta town where I grew up. As adults, we became good friends when we both married and moved to Jackson, Mississippi. My son Sam and her son Andrew are just three months apart in age and have been friends since they were crawlers. Throughout elementary, junior high, and high school, when you saw Sam's red head, you most certainly saw Andrew's towhead close by. They were always cooking up a plan of some sort and have been lifelong friends.

In the spring semester of their junior year in high school, Sam and Andrew went with a group on a college tour. The tour visited numerous schools. After their visit to the University of Georgia, Sam called home and said, "Call off the search. This is the place!" Of course, Andrew loved it, too!

Both boys applied, were accepted, and received academic scholarships to UGA. In addition to UGA being a wonderful school that offered everything the guys wanted, it had the major plus of being located in Athens, a charming small town with a huge music scene.

This music scene was a big draw for both Sam and Andrew. R.E.M. is one of several major bands that got their start in Athens, and they have a song titled "Sweetness Follows." Thus, Sam came up with the title for this book. The title alludes not only to the sweetness of a dessert that follows a meal, but also to the sweetness of friends and the entire communities of Athens and Jackson to our family after Sam's accident. These "Treats of the Week" from Katy were the highlight of every Monday for over a year, and they exemplify the sweet, caring, sustaining support we received from hundreds of people during Sam's recovery. With the recipes now shared in this book, their sweetness will continue for others. Enjoy!

—Leila Lane

The Road to Recovery

During their stay at the hospital in Athens, Sam's parents, Sam and Leila, gave the medical staff a gift—that of their complete faith and trust.

"Sam had faced a devastating injury when I first met him and subsequently the Lane family. Due to the extensive nature of Sam's head injury, the prime function of all the health care professionals during the acute phase was maintaining the best environment for Sam's brain. The purpose was to allow the greatest possible recovery of the injured portion of the brain and to minimize secondary damage to the uninjured or less severely injured brain. It is easy for non-health care people to understand: "We are taking your son to surgery to remove the blood clot in the brain." And also the statement: "We have done all we can." It is very difficult for parents to watch their son get worse and hear: "Sam is going to get worse for the first several days and then hopefully, slowly get better. I think this will result in the best long-term outcome and the greatest intellectual recovery." Maintaining a good environment for an inured brain can look as if the health care professionals are doing little or nothing, although it is frequently more difficult intellectually than the physical task of surgery. The trust that the Lanes held in my advice, the consulting medical staff's advice, and the ICU staff's advice was incredibly difficult for them, yet played a tremendous role in Sam's ultimate outcome. There were many discussions and many questions of the steps being taken. Judgment cannot be measured by a scan or a blood test, only by observation and trust. When there is a trusting relationship between the entire health care team and the family in such a situation, I believe that it leads to the best outcome. The Lanes demonstrated tremendous trust in our team. Certainly seeing Sam when he was back at UGA and learning of his accomplishments has been rewarding to the entire neuro-team in Athens, yet my personal greatest reward was the trust the Lanes placed in my judgment at the time of his injury and the terribly difficult ICU stay in Athens. Establishing a trusting relationship with the health care team has immeasurable benefits, and I will always believe that trust helped Sam."

Dr. Tim Phillips, Neurosurgeon
Athens Regional Medical Center

"My experience with Sam and his family only served to reinforce and renew my love for nursing. I have been doing this for 15 years, and rarely does a family like the Lanes come along. They reminded me of why I love my job. From the start, they included me as one of the family, and we have remained close ever since. So much good has come from this bad situation. For me, it has meant an extended family. We talk or e-mail on a frequent basis. They cared for me during the loss of my mother and never fail to ask about my children. Sam calls me when he is in Athens, and we try to go to lunch to catch up. At his graduation and party that followed, I felt like I was one of the family, and the best part is that I think they did, too!"

Leigh Anne Landers
ICU Neurosurgery

The Road to Recovery

"Sam was named Best Defensive Player of the Year by the district after his senior high school season, when the team won the state football championship title. His accident really hit us hard. I did some physical therapy with him while he was at St. Dominic's Hospital and Methodist Rehab Center. One day I asked Sam if he would come and speak to the team when he was able. I later learned that when I left the room that day, he told his dad that he would go and speak to the team, but when he did, he would NOT be in a wheelchair – that he would walk onto the field. And that is exactly what he did! He got to the field on a hot summer day when the two-a-day practices were in process. The team surrounded him and took a knee. Sam told them that he knew they were working hard, but then went on to tell them what working hard REALLY was. He told them about his accident and that the doctors had told his parents that he would never walk again. He then said, 'I walked out onto this field today, and I also drove my own car to get here.' The team went wild! They knew what it had taken to get him there and clearly understood what he had come to say."

Ricky Black
Head Football Coach
Jackson Preparatory School
Jackson, MS

"It was Christmas Eve of 2007. I was still, in many ways, brand new to the Cathedral – still putting names with faces and people with families. During one of our glorious Christmas Eve services, as I sat in silence listening to the melodious voices of our choir and people as they sang Silent Night, one of my colleagues gently nudged me, pointed to the back of the Church, and excitedly whispered, 'Do you see that young man?' That was my introduction to Sam. And, it was the first time he had come to church without the aid of a wheelchair. There was a noticeable quiet as he and his daddy slowly made their way forward to receive The Holy Eucharist. There was admiration to be sure and a knowing gratitude that this child, so beloved and admired before the accident, was fighting with the same determination and grit that he'd exuded all of his life. On an evening when we reflected on the new life that has come to the world in Christ Jesus, Sam somehow became an outward and living sign of a new way, a new life, with all of its struggles, hopes, fears, setbacks, and accomplishments. What I have learned about Sam since that time is that while he is not physically the same person he was before the accident, he is and will always remain the Sam we've all come to know and love. And in all of this, while life changes around us, sometimes in ways we'd rather not accept, what never changes is the absolute, unconditional, no-strings-attached, undeserved love of God in Christ. Every time I see Sam, I'm reminded of that night and this blessed reality."

The Very Rev. Edward F. O'Conner
Dean
St. Andrew's Cathedral
Jackson, MS

Back in School

"When I first taught Sam he was a sophomore at UGA, taking American literature 1865 to the present. I quickly learned that not only was Sam an unusually perceptive reader and critic of American literature, but that he possessed great spirit and wisdom beyond his years. Teachers (like parents) are not supposed to have favorites—nevertheless I confess that Sam quickly became one of my favorite students in the class. When I saw Hubert McAlexander in the halls we chatted about our students, and I told him that I hoped he would soon get the chance to teach Sam Lane (indeed, he did, and pronounced him one of the most talented students he had taught). In that class I learned that Sam loved Walt Whitman's poetry, so I was delighted when Sam and his roommate (and old friend as I learned later) Andrew Houston signed up for my early American Literature survey, starting with the early Puritan writers and ending with Whitman and Dickinson.

That group of students turned out to be one of the best I have taught, and one class in particular stands out in my memory due to the roles played by Sam and Andrew. We were discussing Thoreau's Walden, and another excellent student in the class was trying to persuade us that Walden was a sham, and that Thoreau's ideals about nature were naive and ridiculous. Sam and Andrew jumped in, and the debate that ensued was a wonderful thing to behold. In the course of the debate we learned that Sam had camped for a week alone in the woods, and could speak to the value of that experience. Sam and Andrew may not even remember this class, but I was reassured that the spirit of Emerson, Thoreau, and Whitman was alive and well.

Sam only needed two further English classes to graduate from UGA. I knew that a degree from UGA meant a lot to him and to his family. We made arrangements for him to complete his final two classes via Skype with myself and another professor in the English department. I know Sam is capable of many things, but I hope he will keep his love of literature close at hand. I was delighted to participate in the graduation events and the ones that followed in honor of him."

Dr. Susan Rosenbaum
Associate Professor of English
University of Georgia
Athens, GA

Dr. Rosenbaum was studying abroad in England at the time of Sam's accident. She knew that Whitman's Leaves of Grass was his favorite book, so she had her husband bring a copy to the hospital. While Sam remained in a coma, Dr. Hubert H. McAlexander read to him from this book. Dr. McAlexander had become not only his Professor of American Modernism but his faculty mentor as well. During Sam's recovery in Jackson at the MS Methodist Rehabilitation Center, Dr. McAlexander was one of his most welcomed visitors.

Graduation

Graduation was held in Athens on Friday, May 13, 2011. The Athens *Banner-Herald* ran a front page story about Sam. They told of his accident and of the multiple brain injuries that he had sustained. "Doctors weren't sure if he would ever be able to think again, much less complete a college degree." they said. They went on to praise his academic accomplishments. In the morning of that day, the English department held their own graduation ceremony, and Sam's accomplishments were recognized from the podium. The room was filled. When Sam crossed the stage that morning there was a standing ovation, thundering applause, and "not a dry eye in the house." Later that evening, he joined about 5,200 other students "between the hedges" in Sanford stadium for commencement exercises.

The following night the Lanes hosted a graduation celebration, complete with dinner and music, to mark that special occasion. It was held in downtown Athens at the Transmetropolitan and was well attended. Friends, family, and medical staff from Athens, Jackson, and numerous other towns joined in the celebration.

There is a longstanding tradition at the University of Georgia. Until you graduate, you do NOT walk under the iron arches leading onto campus. Only after graduation do you make that coveted walk. Andrew had graduated earlier, and we were delighted when he did indeed walk under the arches. At the party that night, I had a poster-size photo with Sam's photo superimposed beside Andrew, as if they were standing together under the arches. I held the poster and read this poem:

We gather tonight in celebration,
Of our own Sam Lane and his graduation.
Hard work and tenacity have brought him to this.
The thought of giving up only made him boo and hiss!
After reading those books and writing all those papers,
This weekend pays tribute to his drive and his labors.
He was looking so smart in that cap and gown,
A degree from UGA has a marvelous sound!
After speeches, diplomas, and graduation marches,
At last he can walk proud under those arches.
And for me, this is really a dream come true,
'Cause now, in those arches, stand Sam and Andrew!

afterword

Sam and the Lane family exemplify the highest purpose of Methodist Rehab Center, to help a profoundly injured young person recover ability and hope in unprecedented ways.

Every step along Sam's recovery has been miraculous. We have the privilege of continuing to work with Sam in therapy and in research. He has an infectious personality, loves people, and loves life. Everyone here dearly loves him, and he inspires us with tremendous hope for all of our patients. Sam has helped us to see that there is hope and potential for each patient—oftentimes more than we would imagine.

I cannot overstate the impact of the Lane family on Methodist Rehab Center. In addition to Sam's recovery and witness, Sam Lane Sr. has helped to raise more than $2 million for our center's Wilson Research Foundation. These funds have helped establish Methodist as one of the top rehab and research centers in the nation. The discoveries we are making through research are leading to better therapies and patient outcomes. The Lane family is squarely in the center of this thriving and evolving legacy.

Chris Blount, Executive Director
The Wilson Research Foundation
at Methodist Rehabilitation Center

A portion of the proceeds from this book will be given to The Wilson Research Foundation at Methodist Rehabilitation Center.

I would ask that when you make a recipe from this book that you would stop and say a prayer for Sam as he continues to improve. I was in a Bible study years ago, and our leader, Jo Lynn Swayze, would end every lesson with this prayer, "And now God, I want to thank you for what you're gonna do." That is my prayer for Sam and for this book, "And now God, I want to thank you for what you're gonna do."

acknowledgments

Thank you to the many friends who helped with this book. Some tested, some tasted, and some typed. I am grateful to you all.

Claudia Addison	Leila and Sam Lane Sr.	Sue Russ
Ruth Bell	Wesla Leech	Robin and Norwood Smith
Leigh Buckner	Julie Levanway	Jessie Smith
Mona Evans	Meridith May	Gayla and Bill Stone
Lanelle Fincher	Betse Parsons	Pam Turner
Jamie Houston III	Virginia Primos	Ree Walden
Rebecca and Jamie Houston IV	Mary Mills and Spencer Ritchie	Tricia and Alan Walters
Jane and Ken Jones	Patty Roper, food stylist	Laura M. Wofford

Thank you to Don Primos and Primos Café and Bake Shop in Jackson, Mississippi, for providing the cookies featured in the Towering Cookies photo (page 16).

Thank you to these artists who generously gave permission for their work to be used in this book:

Bertis Downs, Manager for the band R.E.M.—"We are moved by the love, compassion, dedication and overall grace in this whole project. I speak for the guys and myself in saying that you not only have our permission to use this title, but our blessings as well. In addition, we will help promote this book in any way we can. We wish you the very best."

Janie Davis, watercolor artist of Bottletree Bakery (page 104)—"I am delighted to have my work included in this book. The Lanes have been our neighbors for years, and I am happy to support them in this way."

Adair Cannada, in championship football photo with Sam and Andrew (pages 4 and 97)—"I would be glad for you to use this in your book. When Sam was in the hospital, still in a coma, my mom made an enlarged copy of this photo and took it to the hospital for Sam to see when he woke up."

contents

Cookies 16

Pies & Tarts 42

Cakes 66

88   *Ice Cream Desserts*

104   *Puddings, Cobblers, Cheesecakes, & More*

125   Index

EASY
Fewer ingredients and steps, usually have most of the ingredients "on hand." Uses shortcuts such as a cake mix.

EASY TO MODERATE
Still easy to make, but may involve a step or two such as bake crust first, chill, etc.

MODERATE
Requires a few more steps in making (chill overnight, uses food processor, beat egg whites and fold in, etc.)

MORE DIFFICULT
More instructions involved and judgments ("when mixture has boiled and is an amber color," etc.)
Don't let this make you stay away from making these. They are well worth the extra time and effort.

towering cookies?

"Sam is a national merit scholar and an excellent student. I am sure that if anyone could figure out how this works, it would be Sam!"

—Marsha Hobbs
Physics Teacher, Jackson Preparatory School
Jackson, MS

Cookies

Macadamia "Butter" Cookies with Dried Cranberries

Grandmother Miller's Butter Pecan Crisps

Toffee Butter Cookies

Old-Fashioned Peanut Butter Cookies

Oatmeal Butterscotch Cookies

Fudge Nut Gems • Snowballs

Really Chocolate Refrigerator Cookies

Almond Apricot Shortbread

Crispy Almond Bars

Chocolate Almond Shortbread Bars

Peanut Butter Bars

Caramel Pecan Brownies

Ultimate Chocolate Brownies

Triple-Layer Chocolate Peanut Butter Brownies

Blonde Brownies • Triple Treat Bars

Chocolate Toffee Bars

Blueberry Cheesecake Bars

Orange Bars with Orange Cream Cheese Frosting

Pecan Pie Bars • Raspberry Almond Bars

Macadamia "Butter" Cookies with Dried Cranberries *easy to moderate*

2/3 cup toasted macadamia nuts
1/2 cup granulated sugar
1/2 cup packed light brown sugar
1 egg
1 teaspoon vanilla extract
1 1/4 cups all-purpose flour
1/2 teaspoon baking soda
1/4 teaspoon salt
1/8 teaspoon nutmeg
1/2 cup dried cranberries, chopped
1/3 cup chopped toasted macadamia nuts
1 tablespoon granulated sugar

Process 2/3 cup macadamia nuts in a food processor to a smooth consistency, about 2 minutes. Combine with 1/2 cup granulated sugar and the brown sugar in a large mixing bowl; mix well. Add the egg and vanilla and mix well.

Stir together the flour, baking soda, salt and nutmeg; add to the sugar mixture. Beat on low speed just until combined (mixture will be very thick). Stir in the cranberries and 1/3 cup chopped macadamia nuts. Chill the dough for 10 minutes.

Preheat the oven to 375 degrees. Divide the dough into 30 equal portions and roll each into a ball. Place 1 tablespoon granulated sugar in a shallow dish. Press each dough ball lightly into the sugar. Place the dough balls sugar-side up on a baking parchment-lined baking sheet. Flatten with a fork. Dip the fork in water and press the tops of the cookies again to form a crisscross pattern.

Bake for 8 to 9 minutes or until golden. Remove the cookies and cool on a wire rack.

Makes 2 1/2 dozen cookies

> To toast nuts for additional flavor, preheat the oven to 350 degrees. Arrange the nuts on a baking sheet; bake for 5 to 10 minutes or until toasted and aromatic, watching closely to prevent burning.

Grandmother Miller's Butter Pecan Crisps

easy

1 cup (2 sticks) butter, softened
2 cups packed brown sugar
2 eggs
1 teaspoon vanilla extract
3 1/2 cups all-purpose flour
1 teaspoon baking soda
1/2 teaspoon salt
1 cup chopped pecans, toasted if desired

Beat the butter in a large mixing bowl on medium speed until fluffy. Beat in the brown sugar gradually. Add the eggs and vanilla and mix well. Stir together the flour, baking soda and salt; add to the butter mixture gradually, mixing well. Stir in the pecans.

Divide the dough into three equal portions and shape each into a 10-inch log. Wrap the logs in waxed paper; chill for at least 4 hours.

Preheat the oven to 375 degrees. Unwrap the logs and slice with a thin sharp knife into 1/4-inch (or thinner) slices. Place on an ungreased baking sheet. Bake for 6 to 8 minutes. Remove the cookies and cool on a wire rack.

Note: This dough will keep well in the refrigerator for up to 2 weeks or in the freezer for up to 8 weeks. Thaw before slicing.

Makes about 10 dozen cookies

This recipe was given to me Hattie Miller, the grandmother of my husband, Jamie. Hattie lived in Greenwood, Mississippi, and was just adorable. Jamie said that growing up, every time they went to visit, she had her brown ceramic cookie jar was filled with these cookies. She continued filling that jar long after we were married. The cookies are so light and crispy that it is really hard to stop eating them. We usually say, "Just one more," and then go right on eating.

Toffee Butter Cookies

easy

1 cup sugar
3/4 cup (1 1/2 sticks) butter, softened
1 egg
1 teaspoon vanilla extract
2 cups all-purpose flour
1 1/2 teaspoons baking powder
1/4 teaspoon baking soda
1/2 cup toffee bits or chocolate-covered toffee bits (I prefer Heath toffee bits)
3 tablespoons (or more) sugar

Preheat the oven to 350 degrees. Combine 1 cup sugar, the butter, egg and vanilla in a large mixing bowl and beat on medium for 2 minutes or until creamy. Combine the flour, baking powder and baking soda. Add to the butter mixture and beat well. Stir in the toffee bits. Coat rounded tablespoonfuls of the dough with 3 tablespoons sugar. Place 2 inches apart on an ungreased baking sheet. Flatten with the bottom of a glass dipped in sugar.

Bake for 11 to 13 minutes or until the edges are light brown. Cool for 2 minutes. Cool on a wire rack. Sprinkle with additional sugar while still warm.

Makes 3 dozen cookies

Old-Fashioned Peanut Butter Cookies

easy to moderate

1 cup (2 sticks) unsalted butter, melted and slightly cooled
1 cup granulated sugar
1 cup packed light brown sugar
2 eggs
1 teaspoon vanilla extract
1 cup chunky peanut butter
2 cups all-purpose flour
1/2 teaspoon baking powder
1/2 teaspoon baking soda
1/2 teaspoon salt
1 cup roasted salted peanuts, finely chopped
1/4 cup granulated sugar

Beat the butter, 1 cup granulated sugar and the brown sugar in a large mixing bowl on medium speed until smooth. Add the eggs, vanilla and peanut butter; mix well. Combine the flour, baking powder, baking soda and salt. Stir into the butter mixture just until combined. Stir in the peanuts. Chill for 10 minutes.

Preheat the oven to 350 degrees. Coat heaping tablespoonfuls of the dough in 1/4 cup sugar and place 3 inches apart on a baking parchment-lined baking sheet. Flatten with a fork, making a crisscross pattern. Bake for 15 minutes or until light brown. Cool the cookies on the baking sheet for 5 minutes, then remove to a wire rack to cool completely.

Makes 3 dozen cookies

Oatmeal Butterscotch Cookies

easy

3/4 cup (1 1/2 sticks) unsalted butter or margarine, softened
3/4 cup granulated sugar
3/4 cup packed brown sugar
2 eggs
1 teaspoon vanilla extract
1 1/4 cups all-purpose flour
1 teaspoon baking soda
1/2 teaspoon cinnamon
1/2 teaspoon salt
3 cups rolled oats
1 2/3 cups butterscotch chips

Preheat the oven to 375 degrees. Combine the butter, granulated sugar and brown sugar in a large mixing bowl; beat until fluffy. Add the eggs and vanilla and mix well.

Stir together the flour, baking soda, cinnamon and salt; add to the butter mixture gradually, mixing well. Stir in the oats and butterscotch chips.

Drop by tablespoonfuls 2 inches apart on an ungreased baking sheet. Bake for 10 minutes or until the edges begin to brown. Remove the cookies and cool on a wire rack.

Makes 5 1/2 dozen cookies

The year I made these treats was a presidential election year. For the past four elections, *Family Circle Magazine* has asked the spouses of the candidates to share a recipe for their family's favorite cookie. The magazine then asks its readers to pick their favorite. Each year, the winner of the cookie contest has gone on to become the first lady! This recipe and the recipe for Almond Apricot Shortbread (page 27) were submitted during the election year of 2008. Lelia, Sam's mom voted, and her choice made it to the White House!

Fudge Nut Gems

easy

4 ounces unsweetened chocolate
1 cup (2 sticks) butter
3 cups sugar
4 eggs, at room temperature
1 teaspoon vanilla extract
1 teaspoon almond extract
3 1/2 cups all-purpose flour
2 teaspoons baking powder
2 cups chopped pecans or walnuts, toasted if desired
1 cup (6 ounces) semisweet chocolate chips

Microwave the unsweetened chocolate and butter in a medium microwave-safe bowl on High for 1 to 2 minutes or until melted. Stir until smooth. Pour into a large mixing bowl. Add the sugar and beat on medium-high for 1 minute or until combined.

Add the eggs one at a time, beating well after each addition. Stir in the extracts. Stir together the flour and baking powder. Add to the chocolate mixture and beat on low until combined. Stir in the pecans and chocolate chips. Chill, covered, for 1 hour.

Preheat the oven to 350 degrees. Shape the dough into 1 1/2-inch balls and place 1 inch apart on an ungreased baking sheet. Bake for 14 to 15 minutes or until the tops of the cookies are cracked. Remove the cookies and cool on a wire rack.

Makes 5 dozen cookies

Snowballs

easy to moderate

1 cup (2 sticks) butter, softened
2/3 cup granulated sugar
1 teaspoon vanilla extract
2 cups all-purpose flour
1 cup finely chopped pecans, toasted if desired
1 (12-ounce) package Hershey's Kisses
1 cup confectioners' sugar, sifted

Combine the butter, granulated sugar and vanilla in a large bowl; beat until fluffy. Add the flour and mix well. Stir in the pecans. Chill, covered, for 1 hour. Press a scant tablespoon of dough around each Kiss, covering completely and shaping into a ball. Chill in the freezer for 15 minutes.

Preheat the oven to 375 degrees. Place the dough balls on an ungreased baking sheet. Bake for 10 to 12 minutes or until set but not brown. Cool the cookies on the baking sheet for 1 minute, then remove to a wire rack. Sprinkle with the confectioners' sugar and cool completely.

Store in an airtight container. Roll each cookie in additional confectioners' sugar before serving.

Note: These cookies keep well.

Makes 3 to 3 1/2 dozen cookies

easy to moderate

Really Chocolate Refrigerator Cookies

A chocolate lover's dream!

- 1/2 cup (1 stick) plus 3 tablespoons unsalted butter, softened
- 2/3 cup packed brown sugar
- 1/4 cup granulated sugar
- 1 teaspoon vanilla extract
- 1 1/4 cups all-purpose flour
- 1/3 cup baking cocoa
- 1/2 teaspoon baking soda
- 1/4 teaspoon salt
- 5 ounces bittersweet chocolate, finely chopped
- 1/2 cup finely chopped pecans
- 3 tablespoons granulated sugar

Beat the butter in a large mixing bowl until smooth and creamy. Add the brown sugar, 1/4 cup granulated sugar and the vanilla and beat for 2 minutes or until fluffy. Sift together the flour, baking cocoa, baking soda and salt; add to the butter mixture, beating until combined (mixture may be crumbly). Stir in the chocolate and pecans.

Knead the dough lightly in the bowl to form a ball. Divide the dough in half and place each half on a sheet of plastic wrap. Shape each into a 1 1/2-inch diameter log and roll in 3 tablespoons granulated sugar. Wrap each log tightly in plastic wrap; chill for about 3 hours or until firm.

Preheat the oven to 325 degrees. Slice the logs with a thin sharp knife into 1/3- to 1/2-inch slices. Place 1 inch apart on a baking parchment-lined baking sheet. Bake for 11 to 12 minutes or until the cookies appear dry, but not firm. Remove the cookies to a wire rack and sprinkle with additional granulated sugar; cool.

Note: This dough will keep well in the refrigerator for up to 2 weeks or in the freezer for up to 8 weeks. Thaw before slicing.

Makes 3 dozen cookies

Almond Apricot Shortbread

easy

1 1/2 cups (3 sticks) unsalted butter, softened
1 1/2 cups sugar
2 egg yolks
2 tablespoons amaretto
1 teaspoon grated lemon zest
1 teaspoon grated orange zest
3 cups cake flour (not self rising)
1/4 teaspoon salt
1 egg white, beaten
1 cup toasted sliced almonds
2/3 cup dried apricots, chopped
2 tablespoons sugar

Preheat the oven to 325 degrees. Line a 12×17-inch baking pan with nonstick foil, extending the foil over the edges of the pan.

Combine the butter and 1 1/2 cups sugar in a large bowl and beat until fluffy. Add the egg yolks one at a time, beating well after each addition. Stir in the liqueur, lemon zest and orange zest. Stir in the cake flour and salt until combined.

Spread the dough evenly in the prepared pan. Brush with the egg white. Sprinkle with the almonds, apricots and 2 tablespoons sugar. Fold the foil over edge of the dough to prevent overbrowning. Bake for 25 minutes or until brown.

Turn off the oven and let the shortbread stand with the oven door slightly open for 15 minutes. Remove the pan to a wire rack. Cut the shortbread into 2×3-inch bars while still warm. Cool completely.

Makes 6 dozen bars

easy

Crispy Almond Bars

1/3 cup sugar
1/2 teaspoon cinnamon
1 1/4 cups all-purpose flour
1/2 cup (1 stick) cold butter, cut into pieces
1 egg yolk
1 egg white, lightly beaten
1/2 cup sliced almonds

Preheat the oven to 350 degrees. Line a 9×13-inch baking pan with foil, extending the foil over the edges of the pan. Coat the foil lightly with nonstick cooking spray.

Mix 2 teaspoons of the sugar and a pinch of the cinnamon in a small bowl; reserve. Combine the remaining sugar and cinnamon with the flour in a medium bowl. Cut in the butter with a pastry blender or two knives until crumbly. Add the egg yolk, stirring until combined.

Press the dough evenly over the bottom of the prepared pan. Brush the egg white over the dough (not all will be needed). Sprinkle with the almonds and the reserved sugar mixture; press gently into the dough.

Bake for 15 to 18 minutes or until light brown. Remove the pan to a wire rack and cool for 10 minutes. Lift the bars from the pan onto a cutting board using the foil. Cut into 1×2 1/4-inch bars. Place the bars on a wire rack to cool completely.

Makes 40 bars

easy to moderate

Chocolate Almond Shortbread Bars

This recipe is from the Holiday Potpourri, *a cookbook that was compiled as part of a fund-raiser for First Presbyterian Day School. With its rich fudge layer and abundance of almonds, this recipe takes shortbread to a new level.*

Almond Crust
1 cup all-purpose flour
1/2 cup whole almonds, ground
1/4 cup sugar
1/2 teaspoon salt
1/2 cup (1 stick) cold butter, cut into pieces
1 egg, lightly beaten

Chocolate Topping
1 (14-ounce) can sweetened condensed milk
2 tablespoons sugar
2 tablespoons butter
1/2 teaspoon almond extract
2 cups (12 ounces) semisweet chocolate chips
1/2 cup sliced almonds, toasted

For the crust, preheat the oven to 350 degrees. Combine the flour, ground almonds, sugar and salt in a large bowl. Add the butter and cut in with a pastry blender or two knives until crumbly. Stir in the egg and mix well.

Press the dough evenly over the bottom of a well-greased 9×13-inch baking pan. Bake for 18 to 20 minutes or until light brown.

For the topping, combine the sweetened condensed milk, sugar, butter and extract in a heavy saucepan. Cook over medium heat until the sugar dissolves, stirring constantly. Remove from the heat and add the chocolate chips, stirring until smooth. Remove the pan to a wire rack.

Spread the topping evenly over the warm crust. Sprinkle with the sliced almonds. Cool completely and then chill. Cut into bars.

Makes 2 dozen bars

Peanut Butter Bars

easy

Cookie Base

3/4 cup shortening
3/4 cup creamy peanut butter
1 cup packed light brown sugar
2 eggs
2 tablespoons milk
1 teaspoon vanilla extract
1 1/3 cups all-purpose flour
1/2 teaspoon baking soda
1/2 cup quick-cooking oats

Peanut Butter Frosting

1/3 cup creamy peanut butter
4 1/2 cups sifted confectioners' sugar
1/4 cup (or more) milk
1 1/2 teaspoons vanilla extract

For the cookie base, preheat the oven to 350 degrees. Combine the shortening and peanut butter in a large mixing bowl and mix well. Add the brown sugar and beat until smooth. Add the eggs, milk and vanilla and mix well. Add the flour and baking soda gradually, beating well. Stir in the oats.

Spread evenly in an ungreased 9×13-inch baking pan. Bake 24 to 26 minutes or until a wooden pick inserted in the center comes out clean. Remove the pan to a wire rack to cool.

For the frosting, beat the peanut butter in a medium bowl until smooth. Beat in 2 cups of the confectioners' sugar gradually. Add 1/4 cup milk and the vanilla, stirring until smooth. Add the remaining confectioners' sugar and beat until smooth. Stir in additional milk if needed to reach a spreading consistency. Spread the frosting evenly over the cooled cookie base. Cut into bars.

Makes 2 dozen bars

easy to moderate

Caramel Pecan Brownies

The name of this recipe does not come close to describing the richness and melt-in-your-mouth flavor of these brownies!

Brownies
1 (1-pound) package light brown sugar
1 cup (2 sticks) butter, melted
3 eggs, beaten
2 cups self-rising flour
Pinch of salt
1 teaspoon vanilla extract
1 cup chopped pecans, toasted if desired

Caramel Frosting
1/2 cup (1 stick) butter
1/2 cup packed dark brown sugar
1/4 cup half-and-half
2 1/2 to 3 cups confectioners' sugar
1 teaspoon vanilla extract
Pinch of salt

For the brownies, preheat the oven to 325 degrees. Combine the brown sugar and butter in a large mixing bowl and beat until smooth. Add the eggs; beat well. Add the flour, salt and vanilla and mix well. Stir in the pecans.

Pour the batter into a greased 9×13-inch baking pan and spread evenly. Bake for 30 to 35 minutes or until golden brown. Remove the pan to a wire rack and cool completely.

For the frosting, melt the butter in a medium saucepan over low heat. Add the brown sugar and cook until dissolved, stirring constantly. Stir in the half-and-half.

Remove from the heat. Add the confectioners' sugar, vanilla and salt; beat until smooth. Pour over the cooled brownies. Frosting will set as it cools. Cut into bars.

Makes 2 dozen brownies

Ultimate Chocolate Brownies

easy to moderate

This is an extremely rich and chocolaty brownie. It is well worth the effort!

2 cups (4 sticks) unsalted butter
1 1/2 pounds semisweet chocolate, chopped
6 eggs
2 1/2 cups sugar
2 tablespoons vanilla extract
2 tablespoons strong brewed espresso
1 cup all-purpose flour
1 tablespoon baking powder
1 teaspoon salt
1 cup (6 ounces) semisweet chocolate chips
1 cup walnuts or pecans, toasted and chopped

Preheat the oven to 350 degrees. Melt the butter with the chopped chocolate in the top of a double boiler over simmering water, stirring until smooth. (Or microwave the butter and chocolate in a large microwave-safe bowl on High 2 to 4 minutes, checking and stirring every 30 seconds until melted; stir until smooth.)

Beat the eggs with the sugar in a large mixing bowl on medium-high speed until pale and thick, about 4 minutes. Beat in the vanilla and espresso. Stir together the flour, baking powder and salt; add to the egg mixture and beat well. Add the chocolate mixture and beat on medium speed until combined. Stir in the chocolate chips and walnuts.

Pour the batter into a 9×13-inch baking pan coated with nonstick cooking spray. Bake for 55 minutes or until the top is shiny and lightly cracked, the edges are set and the center is still moist. Remove the pan to a wire rack to cool. Cut into bars.

Note: These brownies freeze well for up to 8 weeks.

Makes 2 dozen brownies

moderate

Triple-Layer Chocolate Peanut Butter Brownies

Brownie and Peanut Butter Layers
4 ounces unsweetened chocolate
1 cup (2 sticks) butter
3 cups granulated sugar
5 eggs, at room temperature
1 1/2 cups all-purpose flour
1/3 cup baking cocoa
1/2 teaspoon salt
1 teaspoon vanilla extract
1/8 teaspoon instant coffee granules, crushed
1 (16-ounce) jar chunky peanut butter

Chocolate Marshmallow Frosting
1/2 cup (1 stick) butter
1/4 cup baking cocoa
1/3 cup milk
10 large marshmallows
1 (1-pound) package confectioners' sugar, sifted
1/2 teaspoon vanilla extract

For the layers, preheat the oven to 325 degrees. Microwave the chocolate and butter in a microwave-safe bowl on High for 1 to 2 minutes or until melted. Stir until smooth; cool.

Whisk the sugar and eggs in a large bowl until smooth. Add the chocolate mixture and whisk until well blended. Stir together the flour, baking cocoa and salt; add to the chocolate mixture and mix well. Stir in the vanilla and instant coffee.

Pour the batter into a greased 9×13-inch baking pan and spread evenly. Bake for 25 to 30 minutes or until a wooden pick inserted in the center comes out clean. Remove the pan to a wire rack to cool.

Microwave the peanut butter in a microwave-safe bowl at 50% power for 2 to 3 minutes or until melted, stirring occasionally. Spread over the warm brownie layer. Chill for 30 minutes or until the peanut butter is firm.

For the frosting, combine the butter, baking cocoa, milk and marshmallows in a large heavy saucepan over medium heat. Cook until the marshmallows melt, stirring frequently. Remove from the heat and add the confectioners' sugar, stirring until smooth. Stir in the vanilla and mix well. Spread over the chilled peanut butter layer. Chill until set. Cut into bars. Store the brownies in the refrigerator.

Note: These brownies freeze well for up to 8 weeks.

Makes 2 to 3 dozen brownies

These layered brownies are incredible! If making just the base brownie, which is delicious on its own, try adding 3/4 cup chopped toasted pecans for a brownie with a "just right" consistency.

Blonde Brownies

easy

This is a great "go-to" recipe because you usually have all the needed ingredients on hand.

2/3 cup butter, melted
2 cups packed brown sugar
2 eggs
2 cups all-purpose flour, sifted
1 teaspoon baking powder
1/2 teaspoon baking soda
1 teaspoon vanilla extract
1 cup chopped pecans, toasted if desired
1 1/2 cups (9 ounces) semisweet chocolate chips

Preheat the oven to 350 degrees. Combine the butter, brown sugar and eggs in a large bowl and beat until smooth. Stir together the flour, baking powder and baking soda; add to the butter mixture and mix well. Stir in the vanilla and pecans. Pour into a greased 9×13-inch baking pan and spread evenly. Sprinkle evenly with the chocolate chips. Bake for 25 minutes. Remove the pan to a wire rack to cool. Cut into bars.

Makes 2 dozen bars

Triple Treat Bars

easy

2 cups graham cracker crumbs
1/2 cup (1 stick) butter, melted
3 tablespoons sugar
1 1/2 cups toasted chopped pecans
2 cups (12 ounces) semisweet chocolate chips
2 (14-ounce) cans sweetened condensed milk
3/4 cup sweetened flaked coconut

Preheat the oven to 350 degrees. Combine the cracker crumbs, butter and sugar in a bowl and mix well. Press over the bottom of a lightly greased 9×13-inch baking pan. Bake for 8 minutes. Remove from the oven and sprinkle evenly with the pecans and chocolate chips. Pour the sweetened condensed milk evenly over the top. Sprinkle with the coconut. Return the pan to the oven and bake for 25 to 30 minutes longer or until the edges are golden brown. Remove the pan to a wire rack to cool. Cut into bars.

Makes 1 1/2 to 2 dozen bars

Chocolate Toffee Bars

easy to moderate

Although there is no "real" toffee in this recipe, the brown sugar crust gives it a rich taste. It is best to make these cookies on a dry sunny day. High humidity (rain) will not allow the crust to be crisp.

1 cup (2 sticks) margarine, softened
   (do not substitute butter)
1 cup packed brown sugar
2 cups all-purpose flour
3 (4.25-ounce) milk chocolate candy bars,
   broken into pieces (I use Hershey's bars)
1/2 cup (3 ounces) semisweet chocolate chips
1 1/2 cups chopped pecans, toasted if desired

Preheat the oven to 350 degrees. Combine the margarine and brown sugar in a medium mixing bowl and beat until smooth. Add the flour and mix well. Press over the bottom of an ungreased 12×17-inch baking pan.

Bake for 15 minutes or until light brown. Remove the pan to a wire rack. Microwave the milk chocolate and chocolate chips in a microwave-safe bowl on High for 1 to 2 minutes or until melted, stirring every 30 seconds. Stir until smooth and silky. Pour over the warm crust and spread evenly; sprinkle immediately with the pecans and press in gently. Cut into bars while still warm.

Cover tightly with foil and let stand for several hours or overnight until the chocolate is set. Store in an airtight container for up to 2 weeks.

Makes 3 dozen bars

My mother made this recipe every year at Christmas to give to friends. When school started in the fall, our teachers were always delighted to have one of the Smith children in class because it meant she would be getting Nancy Smith's delicious cookies at Christmas!

easy to moderate

Blueberry Cheesecake Bars

These bars cut easily and make a beautiful presentation.

Shortbread Crust
3/4 cup (1 1/2 sticks) cold butter, cut into 1/2-inch pieces
2 cups all-purpose flour
1/2 cup packed brown sugar
1/2 teaspoon salt
1 1/3 cups chopped pecans, toasted if desired

Cheesecake Topping
16 ounces cream cheese, softened
2 eggs
3/4 cup sugar
1 teaspoon vanilla extract
1 cup blueberry preserves

For the crust, preheat the oven to 350 degrees. Combine the butter, flour, brown sugar and salt in a food processor and process until the mixture is crumbly. Stir in the pecans. Press the dough evenly over the bottom of a greased 9×13-inch baking pan. Bake for 20 to 24 minutes or until golden brown. Maintain the oven temperature.

For the topping, beat the cream cheese in a large bowl until smooth. Add the eggs, sugar and vanilla and mix well. Spread the preserves evenly over the warm crust. Pour the cream cheese mixture evenly over the preserves.

Bake for 30 to 34 minutes or until slightly puffed. Remove the pan to a wire rack and cool completely. Cut into bars. Store, covered, in the refrigerator.

Note: These bars freeze well for up to 8 weeks.

Makes 2 dozen bars

easy

Orange Bars with Orange Cream Cheese Frosting

This is a nice recipe for a ladies' luncheon or for "tea time" pick-ups.

Orange Bars
1 1/2 cups all-purpose flour
2 cups sugar
1 teaspoon salt
1 cup (2 sticks) butter, softened
4 eggs, at room temperature
2 teaspoons orange extract
1 teaspoon grated orange zest

Orange Cream Cheese Frosting
8 ounces cream cheese, softened
1/4 cup (1/2 stick) butter, softened
1 (1-pound) package confectioners' sugar
2 tablespoons grated orange zest
2 tablespoons orange juice

For the orange bars, preheat the oven to 350 degrees. Combine the flour, sugar and salt in a large mixing bowl. Combine the butter, eggs, extract and zest in a mixing bowl and beat until blended. Add to the flour mixture and beat until combined.

Pour the batter into a greased 9×13-inch baking pan. Bake for 30 minutes or until golden brown and set. Pierce the entire surface with a fork. Remove the pan to a wire rack and cool completely.

For the frosting, beat the cream cheese and butter in a large mixing bowl until smooth and creamy. Add the confectioners' sugar gradually, beating until smooth. Stir in the zest and juice and mix well. Spread the frosting evenly over the cooled orange bars. Cut into bars.

Note: These bars freeze well for up to 8 weeks.

Makes 2 dozen bars

Pecan Pie Bars *easy*

These transport easily and are always a hit with the men!

2 cups all-purpose flour
2/3 cup confectioners' sugar
3/4 cup (1 1/2 sticks) cold butter, cut into pieces
1/2 cup packed brown sugar
1/2 cup honey
2/3 cup butter
3 tablespoons whipping cream
3 1/2 cups coarsely chopped pecans

Preheat the oven to 350 degrees. Sift the flour and confectioners' sugar into a medium bowl. Cut in 3/4 cup butter with a pastry blender or two knives until crumbly. Press over the bottom and 1 inch up the sides of a lightly greased 9×13-inch baking pan. Bake for 20 minutes or until the edges are light brown; cool.

Bring the brown sugar, honey, 2/3 cup butter and the cream to a boil in a saucepan over medium-high heat. Stir in the pecans. Pour over the baked crust. Bake for 25 to 30 minutes or until golden brown and bubbly. Cool completely on a wire rack. Cut into bars.

Makes 2 dozen bars

Raspberry Almond Bars *easy*

These are wonderful to serve year 'round, but they are especially good in the fall.

2 cups all-purpose flour
1 1/2 cups quick-cooking oats
1 cup sugar
1 cup (2 sticks) cold butter, cut into pieces
1 teaspoon almond extract
1 cup red raspberry preserves
2/3 cup sliced almonds

Preheat the oven to 350 degrees. Combine the flour, oats and sugar in a large bowl. Cut in the butter with a pastry blender or two knives until crumbly. Stir in the extract. Reserve about 2 cups of the oat mixture. Press the remaining oat mixture over the bottom of a greased 9×13-inch baking pan. Spread the preserves over the crust to within 1/2 inch of the edges.

Stir the almonds into the reserved oat mixture and sprinkle evenly over the preserves. Press down gently (some of the preserves will show through). Bake for 25 to 30 minutes or until the edges are golden brown. Remove the pan to a wire rack and cool completely. Cut into bars.

Makes 2 dozen bars

watch *out!*

"I unwittingly helped myself to the first piece of the chocolate tart. My hand was met with resistance when Sam stabbed my hand and said, "Father, you're not the kind of man who would steal food from the handicapped are you?" I knew then that his sense of humor was still intact. I just wasn't so sure about my hand!" —Sam Lane, Sr

Pies & Tarts

Sour Cream Apple Streusel Pie

Double-Crust Apple Pie

Blueberry Cream Pie

Lemon Meringue Pie

Lime Cream Pie in Meringue Shell

Strawberry Cream Pie

Fresh Strawberry Pie

Sweet Potato Pie

Classic Pecan Pie

Black Bottom Pie

Dark Chocolate Walnut Pie

Jim's Macadamia Nut Tart

Ultimate Nut and Chocolate Chip Tart

Pecan Tart

Bittersweet Chocolate Tart

Creamy Lemon White Chocolate Tart

Lemon-Lime Tart

Fresh Fruit Tart

Raspberry Almond Tartlets

easy

Sour Cream Apple Streusel Pie

1 refrigerator pie pastry (I prefer Pillsbury)

Filling
3/4 cup sugar
1 cup sour cream
1 egg
2 tablespoons all-purpose flour
1/4 teaspoon cinnamon
1/4 teaspoon nutmeg
1/8 teaspoon salt
1 teaspoon vanilla extract
2 to 3 tart cooking apples, peeled and cut into 1/4-inch slices (3 cups)

Streusel Topping
1/2 cup all-purpose flour
1/3 cup sugar
1/4 cup chopped pecans, toasted if desired
3/4 teaspoon cinnamon
1/4 cup (1/2 stick) cold butter, cut into small pieces

Preheat the oven to 400 degrees. Unroll the pie pastry and line a 9-inch pie plate; crimp or flute the edge.

For the filling, combine the sugar, sour cream, egg, flour, cinnamon, nutmeg, salt and vanilla in a large mixing bowl; beat on medium speed for 1 to 2 minutes or until well mixed. Stir in the apples. Spoon into the pastry shell.

For the topping, combine the flour, sugar, pecans and cinnamon in a bowl. Cut in the butter until crumbly. Sprinkle evenly over the filling. Bake for 25 minutes. Bake, covered with foil, for 10 to 15 minutes longer or until the filling is bubbly. Remove to a wire rack to cool. Chill until serving time. Refrigerate any leftovers.

Makes 8 servings

Double-Crust Apple Pie

easy to moderate

2 refrigerator pie pastries (I prefer Pillsbury)
8 Granny Smith (or other tart crisp) apples, peeled and sliced
1 1/2 tablespoons lemon juice
3/4 cup packed brown sugar
1/2 cup granulated sugar
1/3 cup all-purpose flour
1 teaspoon cinnamon
1/2 teaspoon nutmeg

Preheat the oven to 450 degrees. Line a 9-inch pie plate with one of the pastries. Toss the apples and lemon juice together in a large bowl. Stir together the brown sugar, granulated sugar, flour, cinnamon and nutmeg; add to the apples, tossing to coat. Spoon into the pastry shell. Top with the remaining pastry; crimp or flute the edge. Cut slits in the top. Bake for 15 minutes. Reduce the oven temperature to 350 degrees and bake for 35 minutes longer or until golden brown. Cool 10 minutes before cutting. Serve warm with ice cream, if desired.

Makes 8 servings

Blueberry Cream Pie

easy

This is a pretty blue color and would be fun for the Fourth of July garnished with strawberries!

1 refrigerator pie pastry (I prefer Pillsbury)
1 egg, beaten
1 cup sour cream
3/4 cup sugar
2 1/2 tablespoons all-purpose flour
1 teaspoon vanilla extract
1 teaspoon lemon juice
1/4 teaspoon salt
2 1/2 cups fresh blueberries
6 tablespoons all-purpose flour
1/4 cup (1/2 stick) butter, softened
2 tablespoons sugar
1/4 cup chopped pecans, toasted if desired

Preheat the oven to 400 degrees. Line a 9-inch pie plate with the pastry; crimp or flute the edge. Combine the egg, sour cream, 3/4 cup sugar, 2 1/2 tablespoons flour, the vanilla, lemon juice and salt in a large mixing bowl and beat on medium speed for 5 minutes or until smooth. Fold in the blueberries. Spoon into the pastry shell. Bake for 25 minutes.

Combine 6 tablespoons flour, the butter, 2 tablespoons sugar and the pecans in a medium bowl and mix well. Sprinkle over the pie and bake for 10 minutes longer. Remove to a wire rack to cool for 10 minutes. Chill in the refrigerator until serving time. Serve with whipped cream, if desired.

Makes 8 servings

Lemon Meringue Pie

moderate

1 refrigerator pie pastry (I prefer Pillsbury)

Filling
1 1/4 cups sugar
1/2 cup cornstarch
1/4 teaspoon salt
2 cups water
4 egg yolks
1/2 cup plus 1 tablespoon lemon juice
1/4 cup (1/2 stick) butter, softened
2 teaspoons grated lemon zest

Meringue
4 egg whites, at room temperature
1/4 teaspoon cream of tartar
1/3 cup sugar

Preheat the oven to 450 degrees. Line a 9-inch pie plate with the pastry; crimp or flute the edge. Prick lightly with a fork; freeze for 10 minutes. Line the pastry shell with foil, extending the foil over the edge; fill with pie weights or dried beans. Bake for 12 minutes or until the pastry is set.

Remove the foil and weights. Reduce the oven temperature to 400 degrees. Bake for 5 to 8 minutes longer or until the crust is light brown. Remove to a wire rack and cool completely. Maintain the oven temperature at 400 degrees.

For the filling, combine the sugar, cornstarch and salt in a medium saucepan. Stir in the water gradually until smooth. Cook over medium-high heat until the mixture boils around the edge of the pan, stirring constantly. Cook for 1 to 2 minutes or until thick. Remove from the heat. Whisk the egg yolks in a medium bowl until blended. Whisk about 1/2 cup of the hot cornstarch mixture into the eggs. Stir in the lemon juice, butter and lemon zest; add to the hot mixture and whisk until blended. Heat until the custard boils around the edge of the pan; boil for 1 minute, stirring constantly. Pour into the cooled crust.

For the meringue, beat the egg whites and cream of tartar in a mixing bowl until soft peaks form. Add the sugar 2 tablespoons at a time, beating on medium speed until stiff peaks form. Spread the meringue over the filling, covering completely. Bake for 8 minutes or until brown. Cool completely on a wire rack before cutting. Slice with a knife dipped in hot water.

Makes 8 servings

I made this pie for supper for my family one night. After we had eaten, I was in the kitchen cleaning up when Andrew came in and asked me what was for dessert. I said, "Andrew, we just ate the lemon pie." He replied, "I know, but it wasn't chocolate, so it didn't count." In this sentiment, I think we are two peas in a pod! I knew immediately what would be on the cover of this book after I saw the photo of the chocolate tart.

Lime Cream Pie in Meringue Shell

moderate

This recipe makes a lovely presentation.

Meringue Shell
4 egg whites, at room temperature
1/4 teaspoon cream of tartar
1 cup sugar

Filling
4 egg yolks
1/2 cup sugar
1/3 cup fresh lime juice (3 large limes)
1/4 teaspoon salt
1 cup heavy whipping cream
1 tablespoon grated lime zest
2 or 3 drops of green food coloring
Whipped cream (optional)
Lime slices (optional)
Grated lime zest (optional)

For the meringue shell, preheat the oven to 275 degrees. Coat a 9-inch deep dish pie plate generously with butter. Combine the egg whites and cream of tartar in a large mixing bowl and beat on high speed until soft peaks form. Beat in the sugar 1 tablespoon at a time until stiff peaks form.

Spread the meringue over the bottom and up the side of the prepared pie plate. Bake for 50 to 60 minutes or until firm and creamy white. Turn off the oven and let the meringue shell stand with the oven door closed for 1 hour. Remove to a wire rack and cool completely.

For the filling, whisk the egg yolks in a saucepan until light and pale yellow. Whisk in the sugar, lime juice and salt. Cook over medium heat for 5 minutes or until the mixture thickens, stirring constantly; do not boil. Cool.

Beat the whipping cream in a large chilled bowl to firm peaks; fold in the cooled lime mixture, lime zest and food coloring. Spoon the filling into the meringue shell, spreading evenly. Chill for at least 4 hours. Garnish with whipped cream, lime slices and lime zest.

Makes 8 servings

Strawberry Cream Pie

easy

Graham Cracker Crust
2 1/2 cups graham cracker crumbs
1/4 cup confectioners' sugar
1/2 cup (1 stick) butter, melted

Filling
8 ounces cream cheese, softened
1/4 cup (1/2 stick) butter, softened
2 eggs
2 cups confectioners' sugar
1/2 teaspoon vanilla extract

Strawberry Topping
1 1/2 cups sliced sweetened strawberries, drained
1 cup whipped cream
Sliced strawberries (optional)

For the crust, preheat the oven to 350 degrees. Combine the graham cracker crumbs, confectioners' sugar and butter in a small bowl and mix well. Press firmly over the bottom and up the side of a 9-inch pie plate. Bake for 10 to 12 minutes or until golden brown. Remove to a wire rack and cool completely.

For the filling, combine the cream cheese and butter in a large bowl and beat until fluffy. Add the eggs, confectioners' sugar and vanilla; beat until smooth. Pour into the cooled crust and spread evenly. Chill for 30 minutes.

For the topping, fold the sweetened strawberries into the whipped cream in a medium bowl. Spread evenly over the filling and chill for at least 6 hours. Garnish with additional sliced strawberries.

Note: If you are concerned about using raw eggs, use eggs pasteurized in their shells, which are sold at some specialty food stores, or use an equivalent amount of pasteurized egg substitute.

Makes 8 servings

Fresh Strawberry Pie

easy

1 refrigerator pie pastry (I prefer Pillsbury)
3/4 cup sugar
3 tablespoons cornstarch
Pinch of salt
1 1/4 cups lemon-lime soda
1/2 (3-ounce) package strawberry-flavor gelatin
3 cups fresh strawberries, sliced

Preheat the oven to 450 degrees. Line a 9-inch pie plate with the pastry; crimp or flute the edge. Prick the pastry lightly with a fork. Line the pastry shell with foil, extending the foil over the edge; fill with pie weights or dried beans.

Bake for 12 minutes or until the pastry is set. Remove the foil and weights. Reduce the oven temperature to 400 degrees. Bake for 5 to 8 minutes longer or until the crust is light brown. Remove to a wire rack and cool completely.

Combine the sugar, cornstarch, salt and lemon-lime soda in a medium saucepan. Cook until the mixture thickens, stirring constantly. Stir in the gelatin and mix well. Cool to room temperature. Arrange the strawberries in the cooled crust and pour the gelatin mixture over the berries. Chill in the refrigerator until set. Serve with whipped cream.

Makes 8 servings

Sweet Potato Pie

easy

To make this pie a pretty purple color, use garnet organic sweet potatoes. Perfect for football or Mardi Gras parties!

1 refrigerator pie pastry (I prefer Pillsbury)
2 cups mashed cooked sweet potatoes
1/2 cup (1 stick) butter, melted
1 1/2 cups sugar
1 tablespoon all-purpose flour
1 teaspoon vanilla extract
3/4 teaspoon lemon extract
1/4 teaspoon (heaping) cinnamon
1/4 teaspoon (heaping) nutmeg
3 eggs
2/3 cup evaporated milk

Place a baking sheet in the oven. Preheat the oven to 350 degrees. Unroll the pie pastry and line a 9-inch deep dish pie plate; crimp or flute the edge. Combine the sweet potatoes and butter in a large mixing bowl and mix well. Add the sugar, flour, extracts, cinnamon and nutmeg; beat until smooth. Add the eggs one at a time, beating well after each addition. Add the evaporated milk and mix well. Pour into the pastry shell.

Place the pie on the baking sheet and bake for 55 to 60 minutes or until a knife inserted in the center comes out clean, covering the crust edge with foil the last 20 to 30 minutes if needed to prevent overbrowning. Remove to a wire rack to cool. Serve warm or chilled with whipped cream, if desired.

Note: You may use canned sweet potatoes. Drain before packing in a 2-cup measure.

Makes 8 servings

Classic Pecan Pie

easy

One friend who tested this recipe added the comment, "Everyone needs a good pecan pie recipe, and this is it!"

1 refrigerator pie pastry (I prefer Pillsbury)
1 cup packed brown sugar
2 tablespoons all-purpose flour
1 tablespoon butter, softened
1 cup light corn syrup
3 eggs, beaten
1/4 teaspoon salt
1 teaspoon vanilla extract
1 1/2 cups pecan halves

Preheat the oven to 350 degrees. Line a 9-inch deep dish pie plate with the pastry; crimp or flute the edge.

Combine the brown sugar, flour and butter in a large bowl and mix well. Add the corn syrup and eggs and beat until frothy. Stir in the salt, vanilla and pecans. Pour into the pastry shell and bake for 40 to 50 minutes or until set. Let cool for 1 hour or longer before serving. Serve with ice cream, if desired.

Makes 8 servings

more difficult

Black Bottom Pie

When you have finished making this luscious pie, pour a glass of wine and leave the disaster of a mess in the kitchen until tomorrow! (I originally added this at the end of this recipe for a little humor for the friend who was helping with the testing. She made the pie, loved it, and decided that this step of the instructions should remain!)

Gingersnap Crust

1 1/4 cups gingersnap crumbs
2 tablespoons sugar
1/4 cup (1/2 stick) butter, melted

Filling

2 cups milk
4 egg yolks, beaten
1/2 cup sugar
1 tablespoon plus 1 teaspoon cornstarch
3 ounces unsweetened chocolate, melted and cooled
1 teaspoon vanilla extract
1 envelope unflavored gelatin
2 tablespoons cold water
2 tablespoons bourbon or rum
2 egg whites, at room temperature
1/4 teaspoon cream of tartar
1/4 cup sugar
1 cup heavy whipping cream, whipped

Whipped Cream Topping

3/4 cup heavy whipping cream
1 tablespoon sugar
1 square semisweet chocolate, or
  1 bar dark chocolate

For the crust, preheat the oven to 325 degrees. Process the gingersnap crumbs, sugar and butter in a food processor until combined. Press over the bottom and up the side of a 9-inch deep dish pie plate. Bake for 10 minutes. Cool completely on a wire rack.

For the filling, warm the milk in a medium saucepan over medium heat until bubbles form around the edge of the pan. Remove from the heat. Stir a small amount of the hot milk into the egg yolks. Stir the egg yolks gradually into the hot milk. Combine 1/2 cup sugar and the cornstarch in a medium saucepan; stir in the milk mixture gradually. Cook over medium heat for 4 to 5 minutes or until thick, stirring constantly.

Whisk the melted chocolate and 1 1/4 cups of the custard in a medium bowl until blended, reserving the remaining custard. Stir in the vanilla; spread evenly in the prepared crust. Chill for 45 minutes. Soften the gelatin in the water in a small bowl. Warm the reserved custard over low heat and add the gelatin mixture; cook until dissolved, stirring constantly. Stir in the bourbon; remove from the heat.

Beat the egg whites and cream of tartar in a small mixing bowl on medium-high speed until soft peaks form. Beat in 1/4 cup sugar gradually until stiff peaks form. Cool the custard in an ice water bath, stirring constantly until cold. Fold in the meringue and whipped cream. Spoon over the chocolate layer and chill 2 to 10 hours or until set.

For the topping, beat the whipping cream and sugar in a chilled mixing bowl until firm peaks form. Spread over the pie. Shave the chocolate with a peeler to make shavings or curls; sprinkle on top.

Makes 8 servings

Dark Chocolate Walnut Pie

more difficult

1 refrigerator pie pastry (I prefer Pillsbury)
1 cup sugar
1/4 cup water
3/4 cup heavy whipping cream
8 ounces semisweet chocolate
2 tablespoons butter
2 teaspoons vanilla extract
1 1/2 cups chopped toasted walnuts
1/2 cup heavy whipping cream
1/4 cup chopped toasted walnuts

Place a baking sheet in the oven. Preheat the oven to 450 degrees. Line a 9-inch pie plate with the pastry; crimp or flute the edge. Prick the pastry lightly with a fork. Line the pastry shell with foil, extending the foil over the edge; fill with pie weights or dried beans.

Place the pie plate on the baking sheet and bake for 12 minutes or until the pastry is set. Remove the foil and weights. Reduce the oven temperature to 400 degrees. Bake for 5 to 8 minutes longer or until the crust is light brown. Remove to a wire rack and cool completely.

Combine the sugar and water is a heavy 3-quart saucepan. Cook over medium-high heat until the sugar dissolves and turns amber in color, about 15 minutes, swirling the pan occasionally.

Microwave 3/4 cup cream in a microwave-safe 1-cup measure on High for 45 seconds or until warm. Remove the saucepan from the heat and stir in the warm cream, mixing until smooth (mixture will stiffen when the cream is added). Add the chocolate and butter, stirring until melted and smooth. Stir in the vanilla and 1 1/2 cups walnuts.

Pour into the prepared crust. Cool on a wire rack for 1 hour and then chill for at least 3 hours or until set. When ready to serve, beat 1/2 cup whipping cream in a chilled mixing bowl until firm peaks form. Spread over the pie and sprinkle with 1/4 cup walnuts.

Makes 8 servings

Jim's Macadamia Nut Tart

more difficult

From Jim Hudson at Bon Ami in Jackson, Mississippi—Jim makes his pastry from scratch, but I take the shortcut of using refrigerator pastry. That doesn't detract from his rich, sweet creation—perfect for a special occasion.

1 refrigerator pie pastry (I prefer Pillsbury)
1/2 cup light corn syrup
1/2 cup dark corn syrup
1 egg
1/2 cup sugar
1 1/2 tablespoons butter, melted
1 teaspoon espresso powder
1/2 teaspoon vanilla extract
6 ounces macadamia nuts, chopped
4 ounces white chocolate
2 teaspoons butter
1 tablespoon plus 1 teaspoon water
White chocolate shavings (optional)
1/3 cup chopped pistachio nuts (optional)

Preheat the oven to 350 degrees. Line a 9- or 10-inch tart pan with removable bottom with the pastry; trim the edge. Line the pastry shell with foil, extending the foil over the edge; fill with pie weights or dried beans. Bake for 20 minutes. Remove the foil and weights. Cool on a wire rack. Increase the oven temperature to 375 degrees.

Combine the light corn syrup, dark corn syrup, egg, sugar, 1 1/2 tablespoons butter, the espresso powder and vanilla in a large mixing bowl and beat until smooth. Sprinkle the macadamia nuts evenly over the bottom of the prepared crust. Pour the corn syrup mixture over the nuts. Bake for 45 minutes or until the filling is set. Remove to a wire rack and cool completely.

Combine the white chocolate, 2 teaspoons butter and the water in the top of a double boiler over simmering water and heat until melted, stirring until smooth. Cool slightly, then spread evenly over the tart. Cool completely. Garnish with white chocolate shavings and pistachio nuts. Serve with vanilla bean ice cream, if desired.

Makes 8 to 10 servings

Ultimate Nut and Chocolate Chip Tart

easy

This is really delicious with a scoop of vanilla ice cream served on the side!

1 refrigerator pie pastry (I prefer Pillsbury)
3 eggs
1 cup light corn syrup
1/2 cup packed light brown sugar
1/3 cup butter, melted and cooled
1 teaspoon vanilla extract
1 cup coarsely chopped salted mixed nuts
1/2 cup plus 1/3 cup miniature semisweet chocolate chips
1 tablespoon shortening

Position an oven rack in the bottom third of the oven. Preheat the oven to 350 degrees. Line an 11-inch tart pan with removable bottom with the pastry; trim the edge. Whisk the eggs in a large bowl until blended. Add the corn syrup, brown sugar, butter and vanilla and whisk until smooth. Stir in the mixed nuts and 1/2 cup of the chocolate chips.

Place the pastry-lined tart pan on a baking sheet; pour the mixed nut mixture carefully into the pastry shell. Bake for 30 to 40 minutes or until a knife inserted in the center comes out clean. Remove to a wire rack and cool completely.

To serve, cut the tart into wedges and place on serving plates. Melt the remaining 1/3 cup chocolate chips and the shortening in a small heavy saucepan over low heat, stirring constantly. Remove from the heat and stir until smooth. Cool slightly; spoon into a small, heavy-duty plastic bag. Snip a very small hole in one corner of the bag.

Drizzle the chocolate in a zigzag pattern across the tart wedges, overlapping onto the plates. Serve with vanilla ice cream, if desired.

Makes 8 to 12 servings

Pecan Tart

easy

1 refrigerator pie pastry (I prefer Pillsbury)
5 tablespoons unsalted butter
1 cup dark corn syrup
3/4 cup sugar
1/4 teaspoon salt
3 eggs
2 cups pecan halves
1 teaspoon vanilla extract

Position an oven rack in the bottom third of the oven; place a rimmed baking sheet on the rack. Preheat the oven to 425 degrees. Line a 9- or 10-inch tart pan with removable bottom with the pastry; trim the edge.

Melt the butter in a heavy saucepan over medium heat; bring to a simmer. Cook about 2 minutes or until golden brown, whisking constantly. Cool to room temperature. Whisk the corn syrup, sugar and salt in a large bowl until blended. Whisk in the cooled browned butter. Whisk in the eggs one at a time. Stir in the pecans and vanilla. Pour into the prepared crust.

Place the tart pan on the baking sheet and bake for 10 minutes. Reduce the oven temperature to 350 degrees; bake for 50 minutes longer or until puffed and the center is just set. Remove the pan to a wire rack and cool for at least 1 hour. Serve with vanilla ice cream, if desired.

Makes 8 servings

Bittersweet Chocolate Tart

easy

Another time, use a refrigerator pie pastry for the crust of this tart. Line the tart pan with the pastry and prebake as directed.

1/2 (16- to 18-ounce) roll refrigerator sugar cookie dough
1 1/4 cups heavy cream
6 ounces bittersweet chocolate, chopped
6 ounces semisweet chocolate, chopped
2 eggs, beaten
2 teaspoons vanilla extract
Whipped cream (optional)
Baking cocoa (optional)
Chocolate shavings (optional)
Mint sprigs (optional)
Raspberries (optional)

Position an oven rack in the bottom third of the oven. Preheat the oven to 350 degrees. Flatten the cookie dough on a lightly floured surface; roll out to a 12-inch round. Place in a 9-inch tart pan with removable bottom and press over the bottom and up the side of the pan, folding over any excess to form a thick edge. Freeze for 20 minutes.

Line the dough-lined pan with foil, extending the foil over the edge; fill with pie weights or dried beans. Bake for 25 minutes or until set. Remove the foil and weights. Bake for 10 minutes longer or until golden brown. Remove the pan to a wire rack to cool.

Reduce the oven temperature to 250 degrees. Position the oven rack in the middle of the oven. Microwave the cream in a large microwave-safe bowl on High for 2 to 3 minutes or until barely simmering. Add the chocolates and stir until melted and smooth. Whisk in the eggs and vanilla. Pour into the prepared crust.

Bake for 25 minutes or until almost set. Turn off the oven and let the tart stand with the oven door closed for 30 minutes. Remove the pan to a wire rack and cool to room temperature. Chill for at least 2 hours (or up to 3 days) before serving. If refrigerated for several hours, let stand at room temperature for 1 1/2 hours before serving. Use whipped cream as a top layer or spoon onto individual servings. Garnish with baking cocoa, chocolate shavings, mint sprigs and/or raspberries.

Makes 16 servings

more difficult

Creamy Lemon White Chocolate Tart

Lemon Curd
2 cups sugar
1/2 cup (1 stick) butter, cut into pieces
2 tablespoons grated lemon zest
1 cup fresh lemon juice
4 eggs

Tart
1 refrigerator pie pastry (I prefer Pillsbury)
8 ounces white chocolate, chopped
8 ounces cream cheese, softened
Whipped cream (optional)
Strips of lemon zest, curled (optional)

Combine the sugar, butter, lemon zest and juice in a heavy medium saucepan. Cook over medium heat for 3 to 4 minutes or until the butter melts and the sugar dissolves, stirring constantly. Whisk the eggs in a small bowl until blended.

Whisk about one-fourth of the hot lemon mixture into the eggs; whisk the eggs into the hot lemon mixture. Cook over medium-low heat for about 15 minutes or until the mixture thickens and coats the back of a spoon, whisking constantly. Remove from the heat and cool completely.

Makes about 5 cups

Line a 9- or 10-inch tart pan with removable bottom with the pastry; trim the edge. Prick the pastry with a fork. Chill for 20 minutes. Place a baking sheet in the oven. Preheat the oven to 425 degrees. Place the pastry-lined tart pan on the baking sheet and bake for 15 minutes or until golden brown. Remove the tart pan to a wire rack and cool completely.

Microwave the white chocolate in a medium microwave-safe bowl on High for $1 1/2$ minutes or until melted, stirring every 30 seconds. Stir until smooth. Beat the cream cheese in a large mixing bowl on medium speed until fluffy. Add the melted white chocolate and mix well. Add the Lemon Curd; mix well. Spread evenly in the prepared crust. Chill for at least 4 hours. Garnish with whipped cream and lemon peel curls.

Makes 8 to 12 servings

Lemon-Lime Tart

easy

1 1/2 cups graham cracker crumbs
1/4 cup (1/2 stick) butter, softened
2 tablespoons light brown sugar
1/4 teaspoon cinnamon
1 (14-ounce) can sweetened condensed milk
2 egg yolks
1 teaspoon grated lemon zest
1 teaspoon grated lime zest
1/3 cup fresh lemon juice
1/4 cup fresh lime juice
2 egg whites, at room temperature
Whipped cream (optional)
Strips of lemon and lime zest, curled (optional)

Preheat the oven to 325 degrees. Mix the graham cracker crumbs, butter, brown sugar and cinnamon in a medium bowl. Press over the bottom and up the side of a 9-inch tart pan with removable bottom.

Whisk the sweetened condensed milk, egg yolks, zests and juice in a large bowl until blended and thick. Beat the egg whites in a small mixing bowl on high speed until stiff peaks form. Fold into the lemon mixture. Pour into the prepared crust. Bake for 20 to 25 minutes or until the filling is just set. Cool on a wire rack and then chill for 3 hours. Garnish with whipped cream and lemon and lime peel strips.

Makes 8 to 12 servings

Fresh Fruit Tart

easy

An equally delightful filling for this tart would be Lemon Curd (page 62). It contrasts nicely with the sweetness of the cookie crust. Garnish with kiwifruit and strawberries.

1 (17-ounce) package sugar cookie mix
   (I prefer Betty Crocker)
1/2 cup sour cream
1/2 teaspoon almond extract
1 (4-ounce) package vanilla instant
   pudding mix, prepared
1 cup blueberries or blackberries
3 cups strawberry halves
2 to 3 tablespoons apple jelly

Preheat the oven to 375 degrees. Prepare the cookie mix as the package directs. Press half over the bottom and up the side of a 11-inch tart pan with removable bottom; reserve the remaining dough for another purpose. Bake for 12 to 15 minutes or until golden brown. Cool completely on a wire rack.

Stir the sour cream and extract into the pudding. Chill, covered, until ready to assemble. Remove the tart to a serving platter. Spread with the pudding and top with the fruit. Microwave the jelly in a glass bowl on Medium until melted; brush over the fruit. Chill for at least 2 hours and up to overnight for the best results and a softer crust.

Makes 12 servings

Raspberry Almond Tartlets

easy

1/2 cup (1 stick) butter or margarine, softened
3 ounces cream cheese, softened
1 cup all-purpose flour
1/3 cup seedless raspberry preserves
1 egg
1/2 cup sugar
1/3 cup almond paste, crumbled
1/2 cup whole blanched almonds, coarsely chopped
Fresh raspberries (optional)

Combine the butter and cream cheese in a mixing bowl and beat on medium speed until fluffy. Add the flour; mix well. Chill, covered, for 1 hour.

Preheat the oven to 325 degrees. Divide the chilled dough into 24 portions and roll each into a 1-inch ball. Press each over the bottom and up the side of an ungreased miniature muffin cup. Spoon 1/2 teaspoon of the preserves into each dough-lined cup.

Combine the egg, sugar and almond paste in a small bowl; mix well. Spoon 1 teaspoon of the mixture over the preserves; sprinkle with the almonds. Bake for 25 to 30 minutes. Remove the pan to a wire rack and cool 5 minutes. Remove the tartlets from the pan and cool completely.

Note: Tartlets can be frozen for up to 1 month.

Makes 2 dozen tartlets

from *carrots* to *cake*

I have always been interested in natural and organic foods. These were organic carrots, and they were delicious. Mrs. Houston only made them better when she turned them into carrot cake!

Cakes

Peach Almond Pound Cake

Caramel Pound Cake with Caramel Frosting

Chocolate Pound Cake with Chocolate Glaze

Traditional Pound Cake

White Chocolate Pound Cake

Gooey Chocolate Crunch Cake

Rich Chocolate Bundt Cake with Chocolate Icing

Chocolate Vegan Death Cake

Molten Chocolate Cakes with Mint Fudge Sauce

Red Velvet Cake with Cream Cheese Frosting

White Chocolate Pecan Cake

Caramel Cake

Apple Cake with Caramel Icing

Angel Food Cake with Strawberries

Easy Blueberry Cake

Carrot Cake with Cream Cheese Icing

Sour Cream Coconut Cake

Lemon Layer Cake

Peach Almond Pound Cake

easy

This recipe calls for frozen peaches simply because you can purchase them year 'round. If fresh peaches are in season, they would be even better than frozen.

1 cup (2 sticks) butter, softened
3 cups sugar
6 eggs, at room temperature
3 cups all-purpose flour
1/4 teaspoon baking soda
1/2 teaspoon salt
1/2 cup sour cream, at room temperature
2 1/4 cups frozen sliced peaches, thawed and chopped
1 teaspoon vanilla extract
1 teaspoon almond extract

Preheat the oven to 350 degrees. Beat the butter in a large mixing bowl on medium speed until fluffy. Add the sugar gradually, beating for at least 8 minutes or until smooth. Add the eggs one at a time, beating well after each addition. Stir together the flour, baking soda and salt.

Combine the sour cream and peaches in a small bowl. Add to the butter mixture alternately with the dry ingredients, beating after each addition until just combined, beginning and ending with the dry ingredients. Stir in the extracts. Pour into a greased and floured tube pan.

Bake for 1 1/2 to 1 3/4 hours or until golden brown and a wooden pick inserted in the center comes out clean. Remove the pan to a wire rack and cool for 10 minutes. Turn the cake out of the pan onto the rack and cool completely.

Makes 12 to 16 servings

Caramel Pound Cake with Caramel Frosting

easy

Caramel Pound Cake

1 cup packed dark brown sugar
1 cup packed light brown sugar
1 cup granulated sugar
1 cup (2 sticks) butter, softened
1/2 cup vegetable oil
5 eggs
3 cups all-purpose flour
1/2 teaspoon baking powder
1/2 teaspoon salt
1 cup milk
1/2 teaspoon vanilla extract

Caramel Frosting

1 (1-pound) package light brown sugar
1/2 cup (1 stick) butter
2/3 cup evaporated milk
Dash of salt
1/2 teaspoon baking powder
1/2 teaspoon vanilla extract

For the cake, preheat the oven to 325 degrees. Combine the sugars and butter in a large mixing bowl and beat on medium speed until smooth. Add the oil and mix well. Add the eggs one at a time, beating just until combined.

Stir together the flour, baking powder and salt; add to the butter mixture alternately with the milk, beating on low speed after each addition just until combined, beginning and ending with the flour mixture. Stir in the vanilla. Pour into a greased and floured bundt pan or tube pan.

Bake for 1 hour and 20 minutes or until a wooden pick inserted in the center comes out clean. Remove the pan to a wire rack and cool for 10 minutes. Turn the cake out of the pan onto the rack and cool completely.

For the frosting, combine the brown sugar, butter, evaporated milk and salt in a medium saucepan and bring to a boil, stirring often. Boil for 3 minutes, stirring constantly. Remove from the heat and stir in the baking powder and vanilla. Beat on medium speed for 5 to 7 minutes or until thickened. Drizzle the warm frosting quickly over the cake.

Makes 12 to 16 servings

Chocolate Pound Cake with Chocolate Glaze

easy

Chocolate Pound Cake
1 cup (2 sticks) butter, softened
1/2 cup (1 stick) margarine, softened
3 cups sugar
5 eggs
3 cups cake flour
1/4 cup baking cocoa
1/2 teaspoon salt
1/4 teaspoon instant coffee granules (optional)
1 cup milk
1 tablespoon vanilla extract

Chocolate Glaze
1/2 cup granulated sugar
2 tablespoons baking cocoa
2 tablespoons milk
1 tablespoon light corn syrup
2 tablespoons butter
1 teaspoon vanilla extract
1 cup confectioners' sugar

For the cake, preheat the oven to 350 degrees. Combine the butter, margarine and sugar in a large mixing bowl and beat on medium speed until smooth. Add the eggs one at a time, beating well after each addition.

Stir together the cake flour, baking cocoa, salt and coffee granules; add to the butter mixture alternately with the milk, beating on low speed after each addition just until combined, beginning and ending with the flour mixture. Stir in the vanilla. Pour into a greased and floured tube pan.

Bake for 1 hour or until a wooden pick inserted in the center comes out clean. Remove the pan to a wire rack and cool for 10 minutes. Turn the cake out of the pan onto the rack and cool completely.

For the glaze, combine the granulated sugar, baking cocoa, milk and corn syrup in a medium saucepan; bring to a boil over medium heat. Boil for 1 minute, stirring occasionally. Remove from the heat and stir in the butter and vanilla. Cool for 10 minutes. Beat in the confectioners' sugar until smooth. Pour the warm glaze over the cake.

Makes 12 to 16 servings

Traditional Pound Cake

easy

1 cup (2 sticks) butter, softened
1/2 cup shortening
3 cups sugar
5 eggs
3 cups cake flour
1 cup milk
1 teaspoon vanilla extract
1 teaspoon almond extract
1/2 teaspoon baking powder

Combine the butter and shortening in a large mixing bowl and beat until light and fluffy. Add the sugar and beat for 10 minutes or until smooth. Add the eggs one at a time, beating well after each addition. Add the flour gradually, mixing well. Stir in the milk and extracts. Add the baking powder and mix well. Pour into a greased and floured 12-cup bundt pan (or a small tube pan and a loaf pan) and place in a cold oven.

Turn the oven temperature to 325 or 350 degrees (I bake this cake at 350 degrees.) Bake for 1 1/4 hours without jarring the pan; do not underbake. Remove the pan to a wire rack and cool for 10 minutes. Turn the cake out of the pan onto the rack and cool completely. Serve with sweetened sliced strawberries and vanilla ice cream or whipped cream, if desired.

Makes 12 to 16 servings

This recipe is from *Southern Sideboards*, a cookbook compiled by the Junior League of Jackson, Mississippi. My son, Jamie, insists that this cake is better if I "sweat" it—let it sit, tightly covered, on a cake stand for several hours after it comes out of the oven. I agree that it does make it really moist, but I can rarely wait that long to cut it.

White Chocolate Pound Cake

easy

1 (2-layer) package yellow cake mix
1 (4-ounce) package white chocolate instant pudding mix
1 cup sour cream
4 eggs
1/2 cup vegetable oil
1/2 cup water
2 cups (12 ounces) white chocolate chips

Preheat the oven to 350 degrees. Combine the cake mix, pudding mix, sour cream, eggs, oil and water in a large mixing bowl and beat on low speed for 1 minute. Beat on medium speed for 2 to 3 minutes or until smooth, scraping the side of the bowl (the batter will be thick). Fold in the white chocolate chips.

Pour into a greased and floured bundt pan. Bake for 45 to 50 minutes or until a wooden pick inserted in the center comes out clean. Remove the pan to a wire rack and cool for 10 minutes. Turn the cake out of the pan onto the rack and cool completely.

Makes 12 to 16 servings

Gooey Chocolate Crunch Cake

easy

This is an easy, rich, and luscious dessert!

1 (2-layer) package devil's food cake mix
1/2 (14-ounce) can sweetened condensed milk
1 (12-ounce) jar caramel sauce (I prefer Smuckers)
16 ounces whipped topping, such as Cool Whip
8 (1.4-ounce) milk chocolate-covered toffee candy bars, chopped, or 2 cups toffee bits (I prefer Heath)

Prepare and bake the cake mix using the package directions for a 9×13-inch baking pan. Poke holes in the warm cake with the handle of a wooden spoon. Pour the sweetened condensed milk over the cake. Spread the caramel sauce evenly over the top. Cool completely. Spread the whipped topping over the top and sprinkle with the candy bars. Chill until serving time. Store in the refrigerator.

Makes 16 servings

easy
Rich Chocolate Bundt Cake with Chocolate Icing

If you are pressed for time, you can omit the icing and simply sprinkle the cooled cake with confectioners' sugar.

Chocolate Bundt Cake

1 (2-layer) package yellow cake mix
1 (4-ounce) package chocolate instant pudding mix
1 (4-ounce) package vanilla instant pudding mix
4 eggs
1/2 cup vegetable oil
1 1/2 cups water
1 teaspoon vanilla extract
1 cup (6 ounces) semisweet chocolate chips

Chocolate Icing

1/2 cup granulated sugar
2 tablespoons baking cocoa
2 tablespoons milk
1 tablespoon light corn syrup
2 tablespoons butter
1/2 teaspoon vanilla extract
1 cup confectioners' sugar

For the cake, preheat the oven to 325 degrees. Combine the cake mix, pudding mixes, eggs, oil and water in a large mixing bowl and beat on low speed for 1 minute. Beat on medium speed for 2 to 3 minutes or until smooth, scraping the side of the bowl occasionally. Stir in the vanilla and chocolate chips. Pour into a greased and floured bundt pan.

Bake for 50 to 60 minutes or until a wooden pick inserted in the center comes out clean. Remove the pan to a wire rack and cool for 10 minutes. Turn the cake out of the pan onto the rack and cool completely.

For the icing, combine the granulated sugar, baking cocoa, milk and corn syrup in a medium saucepan and bring to a boil over medium heat. Boil for 1 minute, stirring occasionally. Remove from the heat and stir in the butter and vanilla. Cool for 10 minutes. Beat in the confectioners' sugar until smooth. Pour the warm icing over the cake.

Makes 12 to 16 servings

"My mom has made this cake a lot, and it is my very favorite. I was so glad to see it when it came as the 'Treat of the Week.'"
—Ben Lane, Sam's brother

Chocolate Vegan Death Cake

easy

4 1/2 cups all-purpose flour
3 cups sugar
1 cup baking cocoa
1 tablespoon baking soda
2 teaspoons salt
1 1/2 cups vegetable oil
2 tablespoons vanilla extract
3 cups strong brewed coffee
1/4 cup cider vinegar
1 (12-ounce) package firm silken tofu, drained
3 cups vegan chocolate chips (many semisweet brands contain no dairy)

Preheat the oven to 350 degrees. Grease and flour three 9-inch cake pans. Line the bottoms of the pans with baking parchment or waxed paper.

Sift together the flour, sugar, baking cocoa, baking soda and salt in a large mixing bowl. Add the oil and vanilla and beat on low speed until blended. Add the coffee gradually, beating on medium speed until smooth. Add the vinegar and mix well. Divide the batter equally among the prepared pans.

Bake for 25 to 30 minutes or until a wooden pick inserted in the center comes out clean. Remove the pans to a wire rack and cool for 15 to 20 minutes. Turn the cakes out of the pans onto the rack and cool completely.

Place the tofu in a medium saucepan and mash with a spoon; add the chocolate chips. Cook over medium heat until the chocolate is soft, stirring constantly. Spoon into a food processor and process until smooth. Cool to a spreadable consistency and spread between the layers and over the top and side of the cake.

Makes 10 to 12 servings

This cake was not actually a "Treat of the Week" but was served at the party honoring Sam after graduating from UGA. The cake, and this recipe, came from a restaurant in Athens named The Grit, which specializes in vegetarian meals. This cake is one of Sam's favorites.

Molten Chocolate Cakes with Mint Fudge Sauce

easy

If time does not permit being able to make the Mint Hot Fudge Sauce, these moist rich cakes are wonderful served warm with vanilla or coffee ice cream on the side. Fresh berries and whipped cream are a nice addition also.

Cakes

5 ounces bittersweet chocolate, chopped
1/2 cup (1 stick) plus 2 tablespoons butter
3 eggs
3 egg yolks
1 1/2 cups confectioners' sugar
1/2 cup all-purpose flour
Whipped cream (optional)
Fresh berries (optional)
Mint sprigs (optional)

Mint Hot Fudge Sauce

1/2 cup (3 ounces) semisweet chocolate chips
2 ounces unsweetened chocolate
1/3 cup water
1/4 cup light corn syrup
1/2 teaspoon peppermint extract

Melt the chocolate and butter in a medium saucepan over low heat, stirring constantly. Cool slightly. Whisk the eggs and egg yolks in a large bowl until blended. Whisk in the sugar until blended. Add the chocolate mixture and flour, whisking until smooth. Divide the batter equally among 6 buttered 6- to 8-ounce custard cups or soufflé dishes.

Preheat the oven to 450 degrees. Bake for 11 to 14 minutes or until the sides are set but the centers are still soft. Loosen the cakes with a small knife and immediately turn out onto individual serving plates. Top with the sauce. Garnish with whipped cream, fresh berries and mint sprigs. Serve with vanilla ice cream, if desired.

Makes 6 servings

Combine the chocolate chips, unsweetened chocolate, water and corn syrup in a small saucepan. Cook over low heat for 5 minutes or until melted and smooth, stirring constantly. Stir in the extract. Serve warm.

Makes about 1 cup

Note: These can be made a day ahead; refrigerate, covered, until ready to bake.

easy to moderate

Red Velvet Cake with Cream Cheese Frosting

Red Velvet Cake
1 (2-layer) package red velvet cake mix
1 cup sour cream
3 eggs
1/2 cup vegetable oil
1/4 cup water
1 teaspoon vanilla extract

Cream Cheese Frosting
12 ounces cream cheese, softened
3/4 cup (1 1/2 sticks) butter, softened
5 1/2 to 6 cups confectioners' sugar
2 teaspoons vanilla extract

For the cake, preheat the oven to 350 degrees. Grease and flour three 8- or 9-inch cake pans. Combine the cake mix, sour cream, eggs, oil, water and vanilla in a large mixing bowl and beat on low speed for 1 minute. Scrape down the side of the bowl, then beat on medium speed for 2 to 3 minutes. Divide the batter equally among the prepared pans.

Bake for 20 to 25 minutes or until the cakes spring back when lightly touched and start to pull away from the side of the pan. Remove the pans to a wire rack and cool for 5 minutes. Turn the cakes out of the pans onto the rack and cool completely.

For the frosting, beat the cream cheese and butter in a large mixing bowl on low speed for 30 seconds or until blended. Add the confectioners' sugar gradually, beating until smooth. Add the vanilla and beat until fluffy. Spread the frosting between the layers and over the top and side of the cake. Store in the refrigerator.

Makes 16 servings

I feel so honored every year when my son, Jamie, asks me to make this for the Christmas lunch at his office. Everyone in the office is so nice to him that I am delighted to be a part of their celebration.

White Chocolate Pecan Cake

moderate

White Chocolate Pecan Cake
1 cup (2 sticks) unsalted butter, cut into pieces
3/4 cup water
4 ounces white chocolate, coarsely chopped
1 1/2 cups buttermilk
4 eggs, lightly beaten
2 teaspoons vanilla extract
3 cups all-purpose flour
2 1/4 cups sugar
1 1/2 teaspoons baking soda
1/2 teaspoon salt
1 cup chopped pecans, toasted if desired
1/2 cup all-purpose flour

White Chocolate Frosting
4 ounces white chocolate, coarsely chopped
12 ounces cream cheese, softened
5 tablespoons unsalted butter, softened
3 cups confectioners' sugar, sifted
2 teaspoons vanilla extract
Chopped pecans, toasted if desired

For the cake, preheat the oven to 350 degrees. Grease and flour three 9-inch cake pans; line with waxed paper. Combine the butter and water in a medium saucepan and bring to a boil; heat until the butter melts, stirring occasionally. Remove from the heat and add the white chocolate, stirring until smooth. Add the buttermilk, eggs and vanilla and mix well. Combine 3 cups flour, the sugar, baking soda and salt in a large bowl. Whisk in the white chocolate mixture gradually until smooth.

Toss the pecans and 1/2 cup flour together in a bowl; fold into the batter. Divide the batter equally among the prepared pans. Bake for 30 to 35 minutes or until a wooden pick inserted in the center comes out clean. Remove the pans to a wire rack and cool for 10 minutes. Turn the cakes out of the pans onto the rack and cool completely.

For the frosting, microwave the white chocolate in a small microwave-safe bowl on High for 1 1/2 minutes or until melted; stir until smooth. Cool for 10 minutes. Combine the cream cheese and butter in a large mixing bowl and beat on medium-high speed until light and fluffy. Beat in the melted white chocolate. Add the confectioners' sugar and vanilla and beat until smooth, scraping down the side of the bowl occasionally. Chill for 1 hour or until spreadable.

Spread the frosting between the layers and over the top and side of the cake. Garnish with additional pecans. Chill, covered, for 8 hours or longer before serving. Store the cake in the refrigerator.

Note: This cake also freezes well for up 8 weeks.

Makes 12 to 16 servings

easy

Caramel Cake

Caramel Cake
1 (2-layer) package yellow cake mix
1/4 cup sugar
1 cup sour cream
4 eggs
1/3 cup vegetable oil
1/4 cup water
1 teaspoon vanilla extract

Caramel Icing
1/2 cup (1 stick) butter
1/2 cup packed dark brown sugar
1/4 cup half-and-half
3 to 3 1/2 cups confectioners' sugar
1 teaspoon vanilla extract
Pinch of salt

For the cake, preheat the oven to 350 degrees. Combine the cake mix, sugar, sour cream, eggs, oil, water and vanilla in a large mixing bowl and beat on low speed for 1 minute. Scrape down the side of the bowl, then beat on medium speed for 2 to 3 minutes or until smooth and thick.

Pour the batter into a lightly greased and floured 9×13-inch baking pan. Bake for 30 to 45 minutes or until golden brown and the top springs back when lightly touched. Remove the pan to a wire rack.

For the icing, melt the butter in a medium saucepan over low heat. Add the brown sugar; cook until smooth, stirring constantly. Add the half-and-half and mix well. Remove from the heat. Add the confectioners' sugar and beat until smooth. Pour over the cake. The icing will set up as it cools.

Makes 12 to 16 servings

Apple Cake with Caramel Icing

easy to moderate

Apple Cake
2 cups sugar
1 1/2 cups vegetable oil
3 eggs
3 cups all-purpose flour
2 teaspoons cinnamon
1 teaspoon baking soda
1/2 teaspoon salt
1 teaspoon vanilla extract
2 large cooking apples, cut into 1/2-inch pieces
1 cup chopped pecans, toasted if desired

Caramel Icing
1 (1-pound) package light brown sugar
1/2 cup (1 stick) butter
2/3 cup evaporated milk
Dash of salt
1/2 teaspoon baking powder
1 teaspoon vanilla extract

For the cake, preheat the oven to 350 degrees. Combine the sugar, oil and eggs in a large mixing bowl and beat until smooth. Add the flour, cinnamon, baking soda and salt and mix well (batter will be stiff). Stir in the vanilla, apples and pecans.

Pour the batter into a greased 10-inch tube pan. Bake for 1 hour or until a wooden pick inserted in the center comes out clean. Remove the pan to a wire rack and cool for 10 minutes. Turn the cake out of the pan onto the rack and cool completely.

For the icing, combine the brown sugar, butter, evaporated milk and salt in a medium saucepan and bring to a boil, stirring often. Boil for 3 minutes, stirring constantly. Remove from the heat and stir in the baking powder and vanilla. Beat on medium speed for 5 to 7 minutes or until thickened. Drizzle the warm icing over the cake.

Makes 12 to 16 servings

For an easy, light summertime dessert, prepare *Refreshing Tropical Fruit Cake.* **Preheat the oven to 350 degrees. Grease and flour three 8-inch layer cake pans. Combine 1 (2-layer) package yellow cake mix, 1 (11-ounce) can undrained mandarin oranges, 4 eggs and 1/4 cup vegetable oil in a large bowl and beat well. Divide the batter equally among the prepared pans. Bake for 15 to 20 minutes or until wooden picks inserted in the centers come out clean. Remove the pans to a wire rack and cool for 5 minutes. Turn the cakes out of the pans onto the rack and cool completely. Combine one 16-ounce can crushed pineapple, drained, and one 4-ounce package vanilla instant pudding mix in a large bowl and mix well. Fold in 16 ounces whipped topping, such as Cool Whip. Spread the pineapple mixture between the layers and over the top and side of the cake. Sprinkle 1/2 cup chopped pecans (toasted if desired) on top. Chill until serving time. Store in the refrigerator. Makes 10 to 12 servings.**

Angel Food Cake with Strawberries

easy

- 1 large prepared angel food cake
- 8 ounces cream cheese, softened
- 1 (14-ounce) can sweetened condensed milk
- 1 (16-ounce) package frozen sweetened sliced strawberries, thawed, well drained and patted dry
- 2 cups heavy whipping cream
- 2 tablespoons sugar
- 3 or 4 whole fresh strawberries (optional)

Freeze the cake for 15 to 20 minutes. Combine the cream cheese and condensed milk in a large bowl and beat until smooth. Slice the cake horizontally into 4 equal layers. Place the bottom layer of the cake on a serving plate. Spread with one-third of the cream cheese mixture and top with one-third of the strawberries. Repeat the layering twice and top with the remaining cake layer. Beat the whipping cream with the sugar in a chilled mixing bowl to firm peaks. Frost the side, top and middle of the cake with the whipped cream. Garnish with the fresh strawberries. Chill for at least 3 hours or until set.

Makes 10 to 12 servings

Easy Blueberry Cake

easy

- 1 (2-layer) package butter-recipe cake mix (I prefer Duncan Hines)
- 8 ounces cream cheese, softened
- 4 eggs
- 1/2 cup vegetable oil
- 1 teaspoon vanilla extract
- 2 cups blueberries
- 1/3 cup confectioners' sugar

Preheat the oven to 350 degrees. Beat the cake mix, cream cheese, eggs and oil in a mixing bowl on low speed for 1 minute. Scrape the side of the bowl, then beat on medium speed for 2 to 3 minutes or until smooth and thick. Stir in the vanilla; fold in the blueberries.

Pour the batter into a greased and floured tube pan or bundt pan. Bake for 45 to 50 minutes or until a wooden pick inserted in the center comes out clean. Remove the pan to a wire rack and cool for 10 minutes. Remove to a wire rack and cool completely. Sift the confectioners' sugar over the cooled cake.

Makes 12 servings

Carrot Cake with Cream Cheese Icing

easy to moderate

Over 30 years ago, I worked at First Mississippi National Bank, and we put together our own cookbook called, Cooking the FMNB Way. *This cake was in the collection, and I have been making it ever since.*

Carrot Cake
1 3/4 cups sugar
1 1/2 cups vegetable oil
4 eggs, at room temperature
2 cups all-purpose flour
2 teaspoons baking powder
2 teaspoons baking soda
2 teaspoons cinnamon
1 teaspoon salt
1 teaspoon lemon extract
1 teaspoon vanilla extract
3 cups coarsely grated carrots
1/2 cup chopped pecans, toasted if desired

Cream Cheese Icing
12 ounces cream cheese, softened
3/4 cup (1 1/2 sticks) butter, softened
5 1/2 to 6 cups confectioners' sugar
2 teaspoons vanilla extract

For the cake, preheat the oven to 350 degrees. Grease and flour three 8-inch cake pans. Combine the sugar and oil in a large bowl and beat until smooth. Add the eggs and mix well. Stir together the flour, baking powder, baking soda, cinnamon and salt; add to the sugar mixture and mix well. Stir in the extracts, carrots and pecans. Divide the batter equally among the prepared pans.

Bake for 30 minutes or until the top springs back when lightly touched and a wooden pick inserted in the center comes out clean. Remove the pans to a wire rack and cool for 10 minutes. Turn the cakes out of the pans onto the rack and cool completely.

For the frosting, combine the cream cheese and butter in a large mixing bowl and beat on low speed for 30 seconds or until blended. Add the confectioners' sugar gradually, beating until smooth. Stir in the vanilla and beat until fluffy. Spread the frosting between the layers and over the top and side of the cake. Store in the refrigerator.

Makes 12 to 16 servings

Sour Cream Coconut Cake

moderate

Even though there's no coconut in the cake itself, this luscious creation has been proclaimed "the best coconut cake ever" by more than one taster.

1 (2-layer) package white cake mix
1 cup sour cream
3 eggs
1/2 cup vegetable oil
1 teaspoon vanilla extract
1 (14-ounce) package shredded coconut
1 cup sour cream
1 cup sugar
1 teaspoon vanilla extract
12 ounces whipped topping, such as Cool Whip
1 cup sour cream

Preheat the oven to 350 degrees. Combine the cake mix, 1 cup sour cream, the eggs, oil and 1 teaspoon vanilla in a large mixing bowl and beat on low speed for 1 minute. Scrape down the side of the bowl, then beat on medium speed for 2 to 3 minutes or until smooth and thick. Divide the batter equally into two greased and floured 8- or 9-inch cake pans.

Bake for 27 to 30 minutes or until light brown and the top springs back when lightly touched. Remove the pans to a wire rack and cool for 20 minutes. Turn the cakes out of the pans onto the rack and cool completely.

Slice the cake layers horizontally into halves to make 4 thin layers; place the bottom of one cake layer on a serving plate.

Reserve 2 1/2 cups of the coconut. Combine the remaining coconut with 1 cup sour cream, the sugar and 1 teaspoon vanilla in a medium bowl and mix well. Spread one-third of the coconut mixture over the bottom cake layer. Repeat the layering twice and top with the remaining cake layer. Combine the whipped topping and 1 cup sour cream; spread over the top and side of the cake. Sprinkle with the reserved 2 1/2 cups coconut and press in gently. Chill for 12 to 24 hours before serving.

Makes 16 to 20 servings

In the process of testing these recipes, Ree Walden, in an effort to avoid sugar overload, sent this cake to work with a friend. This is the response he got from one of his co-workers.

"I am glad to tell you the coconut cake was the best coconut cake I have ever eaten. And that is the TRUTH. I normally do not care too much for coconut cake, but this time I will be Mrs. Jack Sprat—I will lick the platter clean!"

Lemon Layer Cake

easy to moderate

You can make a somewhat lower-fat version of this perfect spring or summertime dessert by using reduced-fat sweetened condensed milk, sour cream, and whipped topping.

1 (2-layer) package yellow cake mix
1/4 cup sugar
1 cup sour cream
4 eggs
1/3 cup vegetable oil
1/4 cup water
1 teaspoon vanilla extract
2 (14-ounce) cans sweetened condensed milk
2 tablespoons grated lemon zest
2/3 cup fresh lemon juice
8 ounces whipped topping, such as Cool Whip

Preheat the oven to 350 degrees. Combine the cake mix, sugar, sour cream, eggs, oil, water and vanilla in a large mixing bowl and beat on low speed for 1 minute. Beat on medium speed for 2 to 3 minutes or until smooth and thick. Divide the batter equally into two greased 9-inch cake pans.

Bake for 27 to 32 minutes or until golden brown and the top springs back when lightly touched. Remove the pans to a wire rack and cool for 5 minutes. Turn the cakes out of the pans onto the rack and cool completely.

Combine the sweetened condensed milk, lemon zest and lemon juice in a medium bowl and mix well. Chill for 30 minutes or until thickened.

Slice the cake layers horizontally into halves to make 4 thin layers; place the bottom of one cake layer on a serving plate. Remove the lemon mixture from the refrigerator and reserve 3/4 cup. Spread one-third of the remaining lemon mixture on the bottom cake layer. Repeat the layering twice and top with the remaining cake layer. Secure the layers with wooden skewers.

Combine the reserved lemon mixture with the whipped topping in a medium bowl and mix well. Frost the side and top of the cake with the whipped topping mixture. Store in the refrigerator.

Makes 12 to 16 servings

road trip *goodies*

Sorry... Gone on a road trip!

When Sam was able to resume his studies, he enrolled at Ole Miss, continuing as an English major. Sam had this to say about one of his desserts, "I was headed to Oxford for the weekend. This ice cream dessert was too good to leave at home. I packed it in dry ice and took it with me to share with my friends there."

Ice Cream Desserts

Toffee Chip Ice Cream Squares
Chocolate Brownie with Mint Ice Cream
Giant Ice Cream Sandwich with Butterscotch Sauce
Individual Ice Cream Sandwiches
Mississippi Mud Ice Cream Pie
Banana Split Pie
Snickers Ice Cream Pie
Peach Pecan Ice Cream Dessert with Caramel Sauce
Frozen Almond Crunch
Frozen Viennese Torte

Toffee Chip Ice Cream Squares

easy to moderate

This is another "go-to" recipe. It can be made ahead of time and frozen until needed. You can adjust the amount of ice cream and candy bars to serve more or fewer. This is another one of my mother's recipes that I have been making and sharing for years. If you can't find chocolate wafers, you can use chocolate crème-filled sandwich cookies. Remove the filling before crushing.

2 1/2 cups chocolate wafer cookie crumbs
1/4 cup sugar
1/2 cup (1 stick) butter, melted
2 (1 1/2-quart) cartons vanilla ice cream, softened
10 (1.4-ounce) milk chocolate-covered toffee candy bars, crushed (I prefer Heath)
1/4 cup chocolate wafer cookie crumbs

Hot Fudge Sauce
1 1/2 cups (9 ounces) semisweet chocolate chips
2 tablespoons plus 1 teaspoon butter
1/2 cup sugar
1/2 cup heavy cream
1/4 cup hot water
1 teaspoon vanilla extract
Pinch of salt

Preheat the oven to 350 degrees. Combine 2 1/2 cups cookie crumbs, the sugar and butter in a bowl and mix well. Press over the bottom of a well-greased 9×13-inch baking pan. Bake for 8 to 10 minutes. Remove the pan to a wire rack and cool completely.

Combine the ice cream and crushed candy bars in a large bowl; mix well. Spread evenly over the prepared crust. Sprinkle with 1/4 cup cookie crumbs. Freeze several hours or overnight until firm. Cut into squares and top with hot fudge sauce.

Makes about 16 servings

Combine the chocolate chips, butter, sugar, cream and water in a small saucepan. Cook over low heat for 5 minutes or until melted and smooth, stirring constantly. Stir in the vanilla and salt. Serve warm.

Makes about 2 1/2 cups

easy

Chocolate Brownie with Mint Ice Cream

This is so easy and great to keep in the freezer to serve anytime. Use your favorite flavor of ice cream—butter pecan, coffee, etc.

1 (18-ounce or larger) package brownie mix
3/4 cup chopped pecans, toasted (optional)
1 (1 1/2-quart) carton mint chocolate chip ice cream, softened

Preheat the oven to 350 degrees. Line a 9×13-inch baking pan with foil, extending the foil over the edges. Coat the foil with vegetable cooking spray. Prepare and bake the brownie mix using the package directions, adding the pecans. Remove the pan from the oven to a wire rack and cool completely. Lift the brownies out of the pan using the foil. Remove the foil and cut the brownie into three 9×4 1/3-inch rectangles.

Line a 5×9-inch loaf pan with foil, extending the foil over the sides by 4 inches. Place the ice cream in a large bowl and stir until smooth; refrigerate. Place one brownie rectangle in the bottom of the prepared loaf pan. Spread one-third of the ice cream over the brownie. Repeat the layering twice, ending with ice cream. Freeze until firm. Remove the brownie loaf from the pan using the foil. Cover the top of the brownie loaf with foil and freeze until ready to serve.

To serve, remove the foil. Place the brownie loaf on a cutting board and let stand for about 10 minutes or until slightly softened. Cut into slices and serve with hot fudge sauce.

Makes 8 to 10 servings

Hot Fudge Sauce
1 1/2 cups (9 ounces) semisweet chocolate chips
2 tablespoons plus 1 teaspoon butter
1/2 cup sugar
1/2 cup heavy cream
1/4 cup hot water
1 teaspoon vanilla extract
Pinch of salt

Combine the chocolate chips, butter, sugar, cream and water in a small saucepan. Cook over low heat for 5 minutes or until melted and smooth, stirring constantly. Stir in the vanilla and salt. Serve warm.

Makes about 2 1/2 cups

Giant Ice Cream Sandwich with Butterscotch Sauce *moderate*

For a shortcut, you can use a 16- to 18-ounce roll of refrigerator chocolate chip cookie dough. Divide the dough in half. Press each portion over the bottom of a 9-inch cake pan; bake for 8 to 10 minutes.

Butterscotch Sauce
3/4 cup packed dark brown sugar
1/2 cup dark corn syrup
6 tablespoons unsalted butter, cut into pieces
1/4 cup granulated sugar
1/4 teaspoon salt
1/2 cup whipping cream
1 teaspoon vanilla extract

Cookie
1/2 cup (1 stick) plus 1 tablespoon unsalted butter, softened
1/2 cup packed light brown sugar
1/4 cup granulated sugar
1 egg
1 teaspoon vanilla extract
1 1/2 cups all-purpose flour
3/4 teaspoon baking soda
1/4 teaspoon salt
1 1/2 cups (9 ounces) semisweet chocolate chips
1 (1 1/2-quart) carton vanilla ice cream, softened

For the sauce, combine the brown sugar, corn syrup, butter, granulated sugar and salt in a heavy medium saucepan. Cook over low heat until the sugars dissolve, stirring constantly. Increase the heat and bring to a boil; cook until smooth and thickened. Remove from the heat and whisk in the cream and vanilla. (The sauce may bubble vigorously.)

For the cookie, preheat the oven to 350 degrees. Line two 9-inch cake pans with parchment paper and butter the paper. Combine the butter and sugars in a large mixing bowl and beat until smooth. Add the egg and vanilla and mix well. Sift together the flour, baking soda and salt; add to the butter mixture and beat well. Stir in the chocolate chips. Spoon half the dough into each of the prepared pans and spread evenly. Bake for 16 to 18 minutes or until golden brown. Remove the pans to a wire rack and cool for 10 minutes. Turn the cookies out of the pans and peel off the parchment paper. Cool completely.

Place one cookie top side up in a 9-inch springform pan. Drizzle with 1/4 cup of the butterscotch sauce. Spread evenly with the ice cream and drizzle with 1/2 cup of the sauce. Top with the remaining cookie top side up and press gently. Drizzle with 2 tablespoons of the sauce. Cover and freeze for at least 5 hours or up to 3 days. Cover and chill the remaining sauce.

To serve, remove the pan from the freezer and loosen the side of the pan with a small knife. Remove the side of the pan and let the sandwich stand for about 15 minutes or until the ice cream is slightly softened. Heat the remaining butterscotch sauce in a small saucepan over low heat. Cut the sandwich into wedges and serve with the sauce.

Makes 10 to 12 servings

Individual Ice Cream Sandwiches

easy to moderate

This was not a "Treat of the Week" for Sam, but he did have this for a pregame meal which was served to the football team his senior year. It was such a hit and so easy to make that I thought I would include it. This recipe has a thick layer of ice cream—if you want a thinner layer, use less.

2 (16- to 18-ounce) rolls refrigerator chocolate chip cookie dough
2 (1 1/2-quart) cartons vanilla ice cream, softened

Preheat the oven to 350 degrees. Line two 9×13-inch baking pans with foil, extending the foil over the sides of the pan; grease generously. Press a roll of dough over the bottom of each prepared pan. Bake for 14 to 15 minutes or until golden brown. Remove the pans from the oven to a wire rack and cool completely. Lift the cookie layers from the pans with the foil; discard the foil.

Place one of the layers top side down in one of the pans. Place the ice cream in a large bowl and stir until spreadable; spoon over the cookie and spread evenly. Freeze for 15 minutes. Place the second cookie over the ice cream top side up and press gently. Freeze for 1 1/2 to 2 hours or until firm. Cut into squares with a long serrated knife. Wrap each sandwich in plastic wrap. Freeze for at least 6 hours.

Makes 15 servings

"Sam was named Best Defensive Player of the Year by the district after his senior high school season, when the team won the state football championship title. His accident really hit us hard. I did some physical therapy with him while he was at St. Dominic's Hospital and Methodist Rehab Center. One day I asked Sam if he would come and speak to the team when he was able. I later learned that when I left the room that day, he told his dad that he would go and speak to the team, but when he did, he would NOT be in a wheelchair—that he would walk onto the field. And that is exactly what he did! He got to the field on a hot summer day when the two-a-day practices were in process. The team surrounded him and took a knee. Sam told them that he knew they were working hard, but then went on to tell them what working hard REALLY was. He told them about his accident and that the doctors had told his parents that he would never walk again. He then said, 'I walked out onto this field today, and I also drove my own car to get here.' The team went wild! They knew what it had taken to get him there and clearly understood what he had come to say."

—Ricky Black, *Head Football Coach*
Jackson Preparatory School, Jackson, MS

Mississippi Mud Ice Cream Pie

easy to moderate

Pie
- 1 quart coffee ice cream, softened
- 1 (9-inch) chocolate crumb pie shell
- 1 pint vanilla ice cream with chocolate-covered almonds, softened
- 1 cup heavy whipping cream, chilled
- 2 tablespoons sugar
- 1/4 cup slivered almonds, toasted

Hot Fudge Sauce
- 1 1/2 cups (9 ounces) semisweet chocolate chips
- 2 tablespoons plus 1 teaspoon butter
- 1/2 cup sugar
- 1/2 cup heavy cream
- 1/4 cup hot water
- 1 teaspoon vanilla extract
- Pinch of salt

Spoon half the coffee ice cream into the pie shell, spreading evenly. Spread the vanilla ice cream over the top. Top with the remaining coffee ice cream, mounding in the center. Freeze for at least 3 hours or overnight.

To serve, combine the whipping cream and sugar in a small chilled bowl and beat to firm peaks. Remove the pie from the freezer and drizzle 2 tablespoons of room-temperature hot fudge sauce over the top. Sprinkle with the almonds.

Cut the pie into wedges and place on serving plates. Top each serving with the whipped cream. Microwave the remaining fudge sauce until warm and serve with the pie.

Makes 8 servings

Combine the chocolate chips, butter, sugar, cream and water in a small saucepan. Cook over low heat for 5 minutes or until melted and smooth, stirring constantly. Stir in the vanilla and salt. Let cool to room temperature.

Makes about 2 1/2 cups

Banana Split Pie

easy

2 bananas, thinly sliced
1 (9-inch) graham cracker pie shell
2 pints strawberry ice cream, softened
8 ounces whipped topping, such as Cool Whip
Chocolate syrup
Chopped nuts
Maraschino cherries

Arrange the bananas over the bottom of the crust. Spoon the ice cream evenly over the bananas. Spread the whipped topping over the ice cream. Freeze for 4 hours or overnight.

To serve, remove the pie from the freezer and let stand for 5 minutes to soften slightly. Cut into wedges and place on serving plates. Top each serving with chocolate syrup, nuts and a maraschino cherry.

Makes 6 to 8 servings

Snickers Ice Cream Pie

easy to moderate

It is helpful to freeze the Snickers bars before chopping them. Be sure to make the pieces small enough to avoid a potential dentist visit! If you can't find chocolate wafers, use chocolate sandwich cookies. Remove the filling before crushing.

2 cups chocolate wafer cookie crumbs
1/2 cup unsalted dry roasted peanuts, coarsely chopped
1/4 cup (1/2 stick) butter, melted
12 (2-ounce) Snickers candy bars, frozen and chopped
2 quarts vanilla ice cream, slightly softened
1/4 cup chocolate wafer cookie crumbs

Hot Fudge Sauce

1 1/2 cups (9 ounces) semisweet chocolate chips
2 tablespoons plus 1 teaspoon butter
1/2 cup sugar
1/2 cup heavy cream
1/4 cup hot water
1 teaspoon vanilla extract
Pinch of salt

Caramel Sauce

2 cups sugar
1/2 cup water
1 1/4 cups whipping cream
3/4 teaspoon vanilla extract

Preheat the oven to 375 degrees. Combine 2 cups cookie crumbs, the peanuts and butter in a bowl and mix well. Press over the bottom and up the side of a buttered 9-inch deep dish pie plate. Bake for 10 minutes. Remove to a wire rack and cool completely.

Fold the candy into the ice cream in a large bowl. Spoon into the prepared crust. Sprinkle with 1/4 cup cookie crumbs. Freeze for at least 4 hours. To serve, remove the pie from the freezer and let stand for 5 minutes to soften slightly. Cut into wedges and top with warm hot fudge sauce and caramel sauce before serving.

Makes 8 to 10 servings

Combine the chocolate chips, butter, sugar, cream and water in a small saucepan. Cook over low heat for 5 minutes or until melted and smooth, stirring constantly. Stir in the vanilla and salt. Serve warm.

Makes about 2 1/2 cups

Cook the sugar and water in a heavy saucepan over medium heat until the sugar dissolves, stirring constantly. Increase the heat to medium-high and boil, without stirring, for 7 to 8 minutes or until a deep amber color, swirling the pan occasionally and brushing the sides of the pan with a wet pastry brush. Remove from the heat; add the cream gradually. (The sauce will bubble vigorously.) Cook over low heat for 1 minute or until smooth, stirring constantly. Stir in the vanilla. Cool for about 1 hour.

Makes about 3 1/2 cups

Peach Pecan Ice Cream Dessert with Caramel Sauce *more difficult*

Caramel Sauce
2 cups sugar
1/2 cup water
1 1/4 cups whipping cream
3/4 teaspoon vanilla extract

Dessert
2 1/2 cups crushed pecan shortbread cookies (such as Pecan Sandies)
1/4 cup (1/2 stick) butter, melted
1 cup coarsely chopped pecans, toasted if desired
1/2 gallon peach ice cream, softened
1 cup coarsely chopped pecans, toasted if desired
1 cup pecan halves, toasted

For the sauce, combine the sugar and water in a heavy saucepan. Cook over medium heat until the sugar dissolves, stirring constantly. Increase the heat to medium-high and boil, without stirring, for 7 to 8 minutes or until the syrup is a deep amber color, swirling the pan occasionally and brushing down the sides of the pan with a wet pastry brush. Remove from the heat and add the cream gradually. Cook over low heat for 1 minute or until smooth, stirring constantly. Stir in the vanilla. Cool for about 1 hour.

For the dessert, preheat the oven to 325 degrees. Mix the cookie crumbs and butter in a medium bowl. Press over the bottom and 1 inch up the side of a buttered 9-inch springform pan. Sprinkle with 1 cup chopped pecans and press in gently. Bake for 15 minutes or until golden brown. Cool completely on a wire rack.

Drizzle 1/4 cup of the caramel sauce over the bottom of the cooled crust. Freeze for 10 minutes or until set. Spread half the ice cream over the caramel. Drizzle with 1/2 cup of the caramel sauce and sprinkle with 1 cup chopped pecans. Freeze for 10 minutes or until set. Spread evenly with the remaining ice cream. Freeze until firm. Arrange the pecan halves over the top in concentric circles; drizzle with 1/4 cup caramel sauce. Cover with foil and freeze for at least 4 hours up to 5 days. Chill the remaining sauce.

To serve, remove from the freezer and loosen the side of the pan with a small knife. Let stand for about 10 minutes or until slightly softened; remove the side of the pan. Heat the remaining caramel sauce in a small saucepan over low heat, stirring frequently. Cut into wedges and serve with the sauce.

Makes 12 servings

moderate

Frozen Almond Crunch

This is a "do-ahead" recipe. When this was served to our supper club, they suggested that substituting coffee ice cream for the vanilla would be a nice alternative.

1 cup sliced almonds
3/4 cup sugar
3/4 cup (1 1/2 sticks) butter
1 1/2 tablespoons all-purpose flour
3 tablespoons milk
1/2 gallon vanilla ice cream, softened

Preheat the oven to 350 degrees. Line a 10×15-inch baking pan with foil, extending the foil over the sides of the pan. Combine the almonds, sugar, butter, flour and milk in a heavy saucepan over medium heat and bring to a boil, stirring constantly. Remove from the heat. Spread in the prepared pan. Bake for 7 minutes or until golden brown (do not overbake). Remove the pan to a wire rack to cool; remove the foil and crush the almond mixture into small pieces.

Sprinkle half the almond mixture over the bottom of a 10-inch springform pan. Spoon the ice cream into the pan and spread evenly. Sprinkle with the remaining almond mixture, pressing gently with the back of a spoon. Cover and freeze for 8 hours or until firm.

To serve, remove the pan from the freezer and loosen the side of the pan with a small knife. Let stand for 10 minutes to soften slightly; remove the side of the pan. Cut into wedges and serve with dark chocolate sauce.

Makes 12 servings

Dark Chocolate Sauce
1/2 cup (1 stick) butter
4 ounces unsweetened chocolate
1 1/2 cups sugar
1/2 cup baking cocoa
Pinch of salt
1 cup milk
1 teaspoon vanilla extract

Melt the butter and chocolate in a heavy saucepan over low heat, stirring often. Stir together the sugar, baking cocoa and salt; add with the milk to the chocolate mixture and mix well. Bring to a boil over medium heat, stirring constantly. Stir in the vanilla. Cool, stirring occasionally.

Note: The Dark Chocolate Sauce can be stored in the refrigerator for up to 1 week.

Makes 3 cups

Frozen Viennese Torte

moderate

10 whole cinnamon graham crackers
1 cup slivered almonds
1/3 cup butter, melted
1 quart chocolate ice cream, softened
1 quart coffee ice cream, softened
1 quart vanilla ice cream, softened
2 1/2 teaspoons cinnamon
1/2 cup slivered almonds, toasted

Amaretto Cinnamon Sauce
3/4 cup amaretto
3/4 cup honey
1/4 teaspoon cinnamon

Preheat the oven to 350 degrees. Process the graham crackers and 1 cup almonds in a food processor until crushed. Add the butter, processing until crumbly. Press firmly over the bottom and 1 inch up the side of a 10-inch springform pan. Bake for 10 minutes or until light brown. Remove the pan to a wire rack and cool completely.

Spread the chocolate ice cream evenly over the crust. Freeze for 1 hour or until firm. Spread the coffee ice cream evenly over the top and freeze for 1 hour or until firm. Combine the vanilla ice cream and cinnamon in a large mixing bowl and beat on low speed until blended. Spread over the coffee ice cream. Cover and freeze for 8 hours.

To serve, remove the pan from the freezer and loosen the side of the pan with a small knife. Let stand for about 10 minutes or until slightly softened; remove the side of the pan. Cut into wedges and place on serving plates. Sprinkle each serving with 1/2 cup toasted almonds. Drizzle with amaretto cinnamon sauce.

Makes 12 to 14 servings

Combine the amaretto, honey and cinnamon in a small saucepan. Cook over medium heat until hot, stirring often. Cool to room temperature. Store in the refrigerator.

Makes 1 1/2 cups sauce

This is an original watercolor done by Janie Davis and was a birthday gift to me from Sam. Bottletree Bakery is in Oxford, Mississippi, and is well known for its baked goods. On the card with this gift he wrote, "Your treats rival those at Bottletree any day. I certainly look forward to every Monday. I know this is a strange thing to say, but I wish every day was Monday."

Puddings, Cobblers, Cheesecakes, & More

Sticky Toffee Pudding

Rich Bourbon-Glazed Bread Pudding

Butter Pecan Bread Pudding

Banana Pudding

Blackberry Cobbler

Buttery Apple Crumble

Pecan Pie Cheesecake

Triple-Chocolate Cheesecake

Apple Torte

Raspberry Linzer Torte

Boston Cream Pie

Creamy Layered Chocolate Dessert

Crème Caramel

Custard-Filled Éclairs with Chocolate Icing

Tiramisu

easy

Sticky Toffee Pudding

Don't let the dates in this recipe steer you away. They add a lot of moisture, and you won't even know they are there. With a cake-like texture, this pudding is at its best when served with vanilla ice cream, with the warm sauce poured over everything. This recipe comes from the cookbook, All Good Things, by the Saint Andrews Cathedral members in Jackson, Mississippi.

Pudding

3/4 cup chopped dates
1 cup water
1 teaspoon baking soda
1/2 cup (1 stick) butter, softened
2/3 cup confectioners' sugar
2 eggs
1 teaspoon vanilla extract
1 1/2 cups self-rising flour

Caramel Sauce

1 cup packed light brown sugar
1/2 cup heavy cream
1/2 cup (1 stick) butter

For the pudding, combine the dates and water in a small saucepan and bring to a boil. Stir in the baking soda and mix well. Cool to room temperature.

Preheat the oven to 350 degrees. Combine the butter and confectioners' sugar in a large mixing bowl and beat until light and fluffy. Add the eggs one at time, beating well after each addition. Stir in the vanilla. Fold in the flour and the date mixture just until combined; do not overmix. Pour into a greased 8- to 10-inch cake pan. (I have found that using an 8-inch cake pan makes for a more moist cake with a perfect texture.)

Bake for 25 to 30 minutes or until a wooden pick inserted in the center comes out clean; do not overbake. Remove the pan from the oven and cool for 10 minutes.

For the sauce, combine the brown sugar, cream and butter in a small saucepan; cook until smooth, stirring constantly. Bring to a boil, then reduce the heat and simmer for 2 minutes.

To serve, turn the pudding out of the pan onto a serving platter; cut into wedges. Pour some of the sauce over the pudding, covering completely. Serve immediately with ice cream or berries. Serve the remaining sauce on the side.

Note: This pudding freezes well for up to 8 weeks.

Makes 6 to 8 servings

easy

Rich Bourbon-Glazed Bread Pudding

This recipe was given to me to make for a Sunday school party, and it was an instant hit.

Pudding

3 eggs
1 1/4 cups sugar
1 pint (2 cups) half-and-half
1 cup heavy whipping cream
1 cup milk (I prefer skim milk.)
3 tablespoons butter, melted
1 1/2 tablespoons vanilla extract
1 (24-ounce) loaf white bread, crusts trimmed and bread torn into pieces
1/4 cup raisins (optional)

Bourbon Glaze

1 egg
2/3 cup sugar
1/2 cup (1 stick) butter, melted
2 to 3 tablespoons bourbon (optional)

For the pudding, preheat the oven to 350 degrees. Beat the eggs in a large bowl until thick and pale yellow; add the sugar and beat until smooth. Add the half-and-half, cream and milk and mix well. Stir in the butter and mix well. Stir in the vanilla. Add the bread and raisins and mix well.

Spoon into a greased 9×13-inch baking dish. Bake for 40 to 50 minutes; the center will be slightly sunken.

For the glaze, beat the egg in a small saucepan until thick and pale yellow. Add the sugar and beat until smooth. Add the butter slowly, stirring constantly.

Cook over medium heat until slightly thickened and smooth. Stir in the bourbon. Pour the warm glaze evenly over the hot bread pudding. Serve warm.

Makes 8 to 10 servings

Butter Pecan Bread Pudding

easy

Pudding
4 eggs
4 cups milk
2 cups sugar
1/2 cup (or more) chopped **pecans**
3/4 (1-pound) loaf French bread, torn into pieces
1/4 cup (1/2 stick) butter, melted

Bourbon Sauce
2 cups sugar
1/2 cup (1 stick) butter
1/4 cup water
1 egg
2 to 3 tablespoons bourbon, or to taste

For the pudding, preheat the oven to 350 degrees. Beat the eggs in a large bowl until thick and pale yellow. Add the milk and sugar; mix until smooth. Stir in the pecans. Place the bread in a buttered 9×13-inch baking dish. Pour the egg mixture over the bread. Drizzle with the butter. Bake for 45 minutes.

For the sauce, combine the sugar, butter and water in a small saucepan and bring to a boil. Cook until the sugar is dissolved, stirring constantly. Beat the egg in a medium bowl until thick and pale yellow. Whisk the hot sugar mixture gradually into the egg until smooth. Stir in the bourbon. Serve over the warm bread pudding.

Makes 8 servings

I have two recipes for bread pudding with a bourbon sauce, and what I found when testing these recipes is that everyone had a very strong opinion about the texture of bread pudding. The results were split evenly at 50/50. The Rich Bourbon-Glazed Bread Pudding has a very rich and creamy consistency, and the Butter Pecan Bread Pudding has a more dense texture. Whatever your preference for the texture, both sauces are delicious. My thought on the subject is that whichever one is on my spoon at the time is the one I like the best!

Banana Pudding

easy to moderate

The custard for this traditional Southern favorite is made in the microwave.

Custard
2/3 cup sugar
3 tablespoons cornstarch
1/2 teaspoon salt
3 cups milk
3 egg yolks
1 tablespoon butter
2 teaspoons vanilla extract

Meringue
3 egg whites, at room temperature
1/4 teaspoon cream of tartar
6 tablespoons sugar
1 teaspoon vanilla extract
3 or 4 bananas, sliced
Vanilla wafers (I prefer Nabisco)

For the custard, combine 2/3 cup sugar, the cornstarch and salt in a large microwave-safe bowl. Whisk in the milk until blended. Cook on High for 4 minutes; stir. Cook on High for 4 minutes longer. Whisk the egg yolks in a small bowl until blended. Whisk 1/2 cup of the hot milk mixture into the egg yolks, beating well. Whisk the egg yolks into the hot milk mixture.

Cook on High for 2 to 3 minutes until thickened, stirring and checking the consistency after each minute. Stir in the butter and vanilla and mix well. Chill, covered, for 1 hour.

For the meringue, preheat the oven to 350 degrees. Combine the egg whites and cream of tartar in a mixing bowl and beat until soft peaks form. Beat in the sugar gradually on medium speed. Add the vanilla and beat until stiff peaks form.

To assemble, layer the custard, bananas and vanilla wafers in a deep 8- or 9-inch round baking dish (2- to 2 1/2-quart), repeating the layers as needed and ending with the custard. Spread the meringue over the custard, covering completely to the edge of the dish. Bake for 8 to 10 minutes or until light brown. Remove to a wire rack to cool for 30 minutes. Serve warm or chill for 4 to 5 hours before serving.

Makes 8 to 10 servings

Blackberry Cobbler

easy

6 cups fresh or frozen blackberries
2 tablespoons lemon juice
2 cups all-purpose flour
1 1/2 cups sugar
2 teaspoons baking powder
1/2 teaspoon salt
1/4 teaspoon nutmeg
1 cup milk
5 tablespoons butter, melted
1 teaspoon vanilla extract
1 1/2 cups sugar
2 tablespoons cornstarch
1/2 teaspoon salt
1 1/2 cups boiling water

Preheat the oven to 350 degrees. Toss the blackberries with the lemon juice in a bowl; spoon into a well greased 9×13-inch baking dish. Stir together the flour, 1 1/2 cups sugar, the baking powder, 1/2 teaspoon salt and the nutmeg in a bowl. Add the milk, butter and vanilla and mix well. Spread evenly over the berries.

Stir together 1 1/2 cups sugar, the cornstarch and 1/2 teaspoon salt in a small bowl; sprinkle evenly over the batter. Pour the water evenly over the top. Poke holes in the batter using the end of a wooden spoon. Bake for 1 hour or until golden brown and shiny. Serve warm with vanilla ice cream.

Makes 8 servings

Buttery Apple Crumble

easy

1/4 cup granulated sugar
1/4 cup water
1 1/2 teaspoons cornstarch
1 teaspoon cinnamon
1 teaspoon vanilla extract
1/8 teaspoon salt
11 to 12 cups sliced peeled cooking apples
1 cup all-purpose flour
1 cup packed light brown sugar
1 cup old-fashioned oats
1/2 cup (1 stick) butter, melted

Custard Sauce
3 eggs
1/4 cup sugar
Pinch of salt
2 cups half-and-half
1 teaspoon vanilla extract

Preheat the oven to 375 degrees. Combine the granulated sugar, water, cornstarch, cinnamon, vanilla and salt in a large bowl and mix well. Add the apples and toss gently to coat. Spoon into a well greased 9×13-inch baking dish.

Combine the flour, brown sugar, oats and butter in a medium bowl and mix until crumbly; sprinkle over the apples. Bake, covered with foil, for 30 minutes. Remove the foil and bake for 30 minutes longer or until brown. Spoon custard sauce over the top or serve with vanilla ice cream.

Makes 10 to 12 servings

Whisk the eggs, sugar and salt in a heavy saucepan until smooth. Whisk in the half-and-half; cook over medium heat until slightly thickened, whisking constantly. Remove from the heat and stir in the vanilla. Press waxed paper or plastic wrap onto the surface of the custard and cool. Chill for 2 to 3 hours.

Makes 2 1/2 cups

more difficult

Pecan Pie Cheesecake

Vanilla Wafer Crust
1 3/4 cups vanilla wafer crumbs
1/4 cup packed brown sugar
1/3 cup butter, melted

Pecan Filling
1 cup sugar
2/3 cup dark corn syrup
1/3 cup butter, melted
2 eggs
1 1/2 cups chopped pecans, toasted if desired
1 teaspoon vanilla extract

Cheesecake Filling
24 ounces cream cheese, softened
1 1/4 cups packed brown sugar
2 tablespoons all-purpose flour
4 eggs
2/3 cup heavy whipping cream
1 teaspoon vanilla extract
Whipped cream (optional)
Pecan halves (optional)

For the crust, preheat the oven to 350 degrees. Combine the wafer crumbs and brown sugar in a medium bowl; add the butter and mix well. Press firmly over the bottom and up the side of a 9-inch springform pan. Bake for 6 minutes. Remove the pan to a wire rack and cool. Reduce the oven temperature to 325 degrees.

For the pecan filling, combine the sugar, corn syrup, butter, eggs, pecans and vanilla in a saucepan and mix well. Bring to a boil over medium-high heat; reduce the heat and simmer for 8 to 10 minutes or until thickened, stirring constantly. Pour into the prepared crust.

For the cheesecake filling, beat the cream cheese in a large bowl on medium speed until fluffy. Add the brown sugar and flour and beat until smooth. Add the eggs one at a time, beating well after each addition. Stir in the cream and vanilla and mix well. Pour over the pecan layer. Bake for 1 hour. Turn off the oven and let the cheesecake stand with the oven door closed for 1 hour.

Cool completely on a wire rack. Chill for 4 hours or longer before serving. Loosen the edge of the pan with a small knife. Remove the side of the pan and garnish the cheesecake with whipped cream and pecan halves.

Note: This cheesecake freezes well for up to 8 weeks.

Makes 12 to 16 servings

Triple-Chocolate Cheesecake

more difficult

A chocolate crust, chocolate filling made with three types of chocolate, and a chocolate glaze make this a chocolate lover's dream come true. This beautiful dessert would be especially nice for Valentine's Day garnished with whipped cream and strawberries.

Cheesecake
3 tablespoons unsalted butter, melted
1 1/4 cups chocolate wafer cookie crumbs
32 ounces cream cheese, softened
1 3/4 cups sugar
4 eggs
3/4 cup heavy cream
4 ounces milk chocolate, melted and cooled
4 ounces white chocolate, melted and cooled
4 ounces semisweet chocolate, melted and cooled

Chocolate Glaze
4 ounces bittersweet or semisweet chocolate
1/2 cup heavy cream
1/3 cup toasted sliced almonds (optional)

For the cheesecake, preheat the oven to 350 degrees. Combine the butter and crumbs in a bowl and mix well. Press over the bottom of a 9-inch springform pan. Bake for 8 to 10 minutes or until set. Cool on a wire rack. Reduce the oven temperature to 325 degrees. Butter the springform pan. Wrap the outside of the pan with foil and chill. Beat the cream cheese in a bowl for 2 to 3 minutes or until fluffy. Beat in the sugar gradually until smooth. Add the eggs one at a time, beating after each addition. Add the cream and mix well. Place 2 1/2 cups of the filling into each of 3 bowls.

Stir the milk chocolate into one bowl, the white chocolate into the second bowl and the semisweet chocolate into the third bowl. Spread the milk chocolate mixture evenly over the prepared crust. Pour the white chocolate mixture evenly over the top, being careful not to mix the fillings. Spread the semisweet chocolate mixture over the top. Place the springform pan in the center of a large roasting pan. Pour boiling water into the roasting pan to reach halfway up the side of the springform pan. Bake for 2 hours or until set. Turn off the oven; let stand with the oven door closed for 1 hour. Cool on a wire rack. Remove the foil; chill, covered, for 8 hours or overnight.

For the glaze, place the chocolate in a bowl. Heat the cream to a gentle boil in a saucepan; pour over the chocolate. Let stand for 1 minute; whisk until smooth. Pour over the cheesecake and spread to the edge. Chill for 30 minutes. Remove the side of the pan carefully and place the cheesecake on a serving platter. Let stand for 30 minutes. Garnish with the almonds. Cut into wedges with a large knife, wiping the blade clean and dipping in warm water between slices.

Makes 12 to 16 servings

moderate

Apple Torte

1/2 cup (1 stick) butter, softened
1/3 cup sugar
1 teaspoon vanilla extract
1 cup all-purpose flour
8 ounces cream cheese, softened
1/4 cup sugar
1 egg
1 teaspoon vanilla extract
1/3 cup sugar
1/2 teaspoon cinnamon
4 cups sliced peeled cooking apples
1/3 cup sliced almonds
Sweetened whipped cream (optional)
1/3 cup sliced almonds, toasted (optional)

Preheat the oven to 450 degrees. Combine the butter, 1/3 cup sugar and 1 teaspoon vanilla in a bowl and beat until smooth. Stir in the flour and mix well. Press over the bottom and 1 1/2 inches up the side of a 9-inch springform pan.

Combine the cream cheese and 1/4 cup sugar in a bowl and beat until fluffy. Add the egg and 1 teaspoon vanilla and mix well. Spread evenly over the crust.

Combine 1/3 cup sugar and the cinnamon in a large bowl; add the apples and toss to coat. Spread the apples evenly over the cream cheese layer. Sprinkle with 1/3 cup untoasted almonds. Bake for 10 minutes. Reduce the oven temperature to 400 degrees and bake for 25 minutes longer.

Remove the pan to a wire rack and loosen the edge of the pan with a small knife. Cool completely; remove the side of the pan. Garnish with whipped cream and toasted almonds.

Makes 8 to 12 servings

Raspberry Linzer Torte

more difficult

Makes a beautiful presentation.

2/3 cup granulated sugar
Dash of salt
2/3 cup cold butter, cut into pieces
1 egg yolk
1 1/2 teaspoons grated lemon zest
3/4 teaspoon vanilla extract
1 3/4 cups ground almonds
1 1/3 cups all-purpose flour
1/4 teaspoon cinnamon
1/8 teaspoon nutmeg
Pinch of ground cloves
2 (10-ounce) jars black raspberry or red raspberry preserves
1 egg white
1 teaspoon water
Confectioners' sugar, sifted
2 cups heavy whipping cream
2 tablespoons confectioners' sugar

Combine the granulated sugar and salt in a bowl. Cut in the butter with a pastry blender until crumbly. Add the egg yolk, zest and vanilla and mix well. Combine the almonds, flour and spices in a bowl. Add to the butter mixture 1 cup at a time, cutting in each addition until crumbly.

Press 2 1/2 cups of the crumb mixture over the bottom and up the side of a 11-inch tart pan with removable bottom. Shape the remaining crumb mixture into a ball; flatten into a thick disc. Cover and chill the pastry shell and the disc for 2 hours or overnight. Spoon the preserves evenly into the pastry shell and chill.

Roll the pastry disc into a 12-inch round between 2 sheets of lightly floured waxed paper. Cut into 1/2-inch wide strips with a fluted pastry cutter or knife. Freeze for 15 minutes or until firm. Preheat the oven to 400 degrees. Arrange the strips 1 inch apart in a lattice pattern over the preserves; trim the edges.

Beat the egg white and water in a small bowl; brush on the lattice strips. Place the tart pan on a baking sheet and bake for 15 minutes. Reduce the oven temperature to 350 degrees and bake for 20 to 25 minutes longer or until the pastry is brown and the filling is bubbly, covering with foil if the pastry browns too quickly. Remove the pan to a wire rack and cool completely. Remove the side of the pan. Dust with confectioners' sugar.

Beat the cream in a chilled mixing bowl to soft peaks. Add 2 tablespoons confectioners' sugar and beat to firm peaks. Serve over the torte.

Makes 12 servings

Boston Cream Pie

easy to moderate

Cake
1 (2-layer) package yellow cake mix
1/4 cup sugar
1 cup sour cream
4 eggs, at room temperature
1/3 cup vegetable oil
1/4 cup water
1 teaspoon vanilla extract

Custard Filling
2/3 cup sugar
3 tablespoons cornstarch
1/2 teaspoon salt
3 cups milk
3 egg yolks
1 tablespoon butter
2 teaspoons vanilla extract

Chocolate Icing
1 cup granulated sugar
1/4 cup baking cocoa
1/4 cup milk
2 tablespoons light corn syrup
1/4 cup (1/2 stick) butter
1 teaspoon vanilla extract
1 to 1 1/4 cups confectioners' sugar

For the cake, preheat the oven to 350 degrees. Line a 9×13-inch baking pan with foil, extending the foil over the edges. Coat with nonstick cooking spray. Combine the cake ingredients in a large mixing bowl and beat on low speed for 1 minute. Scrape down the side of the bowl; beat on medium speed for 2 to 3 minutes or until smooth and thick. Pour into the prepared pan. Bake for 30 to 45 minutes or until the cake tests done. Cool on a wire rack. Chill for 1 hour. Lift the cake from the pan with the foil and remove the foil. Slice the cake horizontally into 2 thin layers. Place the bottom cake layer back into the pan.

For the filling, combine the sugar, cornstarch and salt in a large microwave-safe bowl. Whisk in the milk until blended. Cook on High for 8 minutes, stirring after 4 minutes. Whisk the egg yolks in a small bowl until blended. Whisk in 1/2 cup of the hot milk mixture. Whisk the egg yolks into the hot milk mixture. Cook on High for 2 to 3 minutes until thickened, stirring and checking the consistency every minute. Stir in the butter and vanilla. Chill, covered, for 2 to 3 hours.

For the icing, combine the granulated sugar and baking cocoa in a saucepan. Add the milk and corn syrup and mix well. Bring to a gentle rolling boil. Boil for 1 minute, stirring constantly. Remove from the heat; stir in the butter and vanilla. Cool for 10 minutes, then beat in the confectioners' sugar until thickened but pourable. Spread desired amount of the custard filling over the cake and top with the remaining cake layer. Spread the icing over the top. Chill for at least 2 hours or overnight before serving.

Makes 12 servings

Note: This recipe freezes well for up to 8 weeks.

easy

Creamy Layered Chocolate Dessert

This is always a crowd pleaser for all ages—kids to seniors!

1 cup self-rising flour
1/2 cup (1 stick) butter, melted
8 ounces cream cheese, softened
12 ounces whipped topping, such as Cool Whip
1 cup confectioners' sugar
2 (4-ounce) boxes chocolate instant pudding mix
1 chocolate bar (optional)

Preheat the oven to 350 degrees. Combine the flour and butter in a small bowl and mix well. Press over the bottom of a 9×13-inch baking pan. Bake for 15 minutes or until light brown. Remove the pan to a wire rack and cool completely.

Combine the cream cheese, 1 cup of the whipped topping and the confectioners' sugar in a medium bowl and beat until smooth. Spread evenly over the cooled crust.

Prepare the pudding mix using the package directions; pour over the cream cheese layer. Spread the remaining whipped topping over the pudding. Shave the chocolate bar with a vegetable peeler to make shavings or curls; sprinkle over the top to garnish.

Makes 12 servings

Crème Caramel

moderate

1/2 cup sugar
5 eggs
1/2 cup sugar
1/4 teaspoon salt
3 cups milk
1 teaspoon vanilla extract
8 strawberries (optional)

Preheat the oven to 350 degrees. Butter eight 6-ounce custard cups. Cook 1/2 cup sugar with 2 or 3 drops of water in a small skillet over medium heat until the sugar melts. Cook until light brown, stirring constantly. Pour the syrup equally into the prepared custard cups. Place the cups in a large baking pan.

Beat the eggs, 1/2 cup sugar and the salt in a mixing bowl on low speed until thick and pale yellow. Add the milk gradually and mix well. Stir in the vanilla. Allow the bubbles to settle, then pour equally into the custard cups.

Pour hot water into the baking pan to within 1 inch of the top of the custard cups. Bake for 1 hour or until a knife inserted in the center comes out clean. Remove the cups to a wire rack and cool for 20 minutes. Loosen the edge of the custards with a small knife. Invert onto individual serving plates. Top with the whipped cream and garnish each serving with a strawberry on the side.

Makes 8 servings

Sweetened Whipped Cream
1 cup heavy whipping cream
1 tablespoon sugar

Beat the cream in a large chilled mixing bowl to soft peaks. Add the sugar gradually and beat to firm peaks.

Makes 2 cups

more difficult

Custard-Filled Éclairs with Chocolate Icing

Eclairs
1 cup all-purpose flour
1 tablespoon sugar
1/8 teaspoon salt
1 cup milk
1/3 cup butter
4 eggs, at room temperature

Preheat the oven to 400 degrees. Sift together the flour, sugar and salt. Bring the milk and butter to a boil in a heavy saucepan over medium-high heat. Add the flour mixture, stirring quickly with a wooden spoon. Cook until the mixture becomes smooth and dry and pulls away from the side of the pan, stirring faster as it cooks. Remove from the heat when the spoon leaves a slight imprint. Cool for 2 minutes.

Add the eggs one at a time, beating vigorously after each addition. Continue beating until the dough is firm and no longer looks wet. Use a pastry bag or a spoon to shape the dough into 2×4-inch tube shapes 2 inches apart on a greased baking sheet. Sprinkle very lightly with water. Bake for 10 minutes. Reduce the oven temperature to 350 degrees and bake for 25 minutes longer or until light brown and firm to the touch.

Remove the éclairs to a wire rack and cool completely. Split horizontally with a sharp knife; remove any moist dough inside the éclairs. Fill with the custard and spread the icing gently over the tops.

Makes 8 to 12 servings

Microwave Custard

2/3 cup granulated sugar
3 tablespoons cornstarch
1/2 teaspoon salt
3 cups milk
3 egg yolks
1 tablespoon butter
2 teaspoons vanilla extract

Combine the sugar, cornstarch and salt in a large microwave-safe bowl. Whisk in the milk until blended. Cook on High for 4 minutes; stir. Cook on High for 4 minutes longer. Whisk the egg yolks in a small bowl until blended. Whisk 1/2 cup of the hot milk mixture into the egg yolks, beating well. Whisk the egg yolks into the hot milk mixture. Cook on High for 2 to 3 minutes until thickened, stirring and checking the consistency after each minute. Stir in the butter and vanilla and mix well. Chill, covered, for 2 to 3 hours.

Makes about 4 cups

Chocolate Icing

1/2 cup granulated sugar
2 tablespoons baking cocoa
2 tablespoons (or more) milk
2 tablespoons light corn syrup
2 tablespoons butter
1/2 teaspoon vanilla extract
1 cup confectioners' sugar

Combine the granulated sugar, baking cocoa, milk and corn syrup in a saucepan and bring to a boil over medium heat. Boil for 1 minute, stirring occasionally. Remove from the heat and stir in the butter and vanilla. Cool for 10 minutes. Beat in the confectioners' sugar until smooth. Add additional milk if the icing gets too thick.

Makes 2 cups

easy to moderate

Tiramisu

Espresso Syrup

1/2 cup sugar
1/3 cup water
2/3 cup strong brewed espresso
1/4 cup Italian or domestic brandy or strong brewed espresso

Tiramisu

1 1/2 cups heavy whipping cream
1/3 cup sugar
2 teaspoons vanilla extract
1 pound mascarpone cheese, softened
8 ounces ladyfingers, biscotti di Savoiardi (Italian ladyfingers) or sponge cake strips
Baking cocoa (optional)

For the syrup, combine the sugar and water in a small saucepan and bring to a boil. Cook until the sugar is dissolved, stirring occasionally. Remove from the heat; cool. Stir in the coffee and brandy.

For the tiramisu, combine the whipping cream and sugar in a small chilled bowl and beat to soft peaks. And the vanilla and beat to firm peaks. Beat the mascarpone cheese in a large bowl until fluffy. Fold in the whipped cream. Place a layer of ladyfingers in the bottom of a 9×13-inch baking dish. Sprinkle with half the syrup. Spread half the mascarpone cheese mixture evenly over the top. Repeat the layering of ladyfingers, syrup and cheese mixture once.

Cover with plastic wrap and chill for at least 6 hours or up to 24 hours. Shake baking cocoa through a fine strainer over the top to garnish before serving.

Note: This dessert freezes well for up to 8 weeks. You may substitute 14 ounces cream cheese plus 2 tablespoons sour cream for the mascarpone.

Makes 12 servings

index

Almonds
Almond Apricot Shortbread, 27
Almond Crust, 30
Apple Torte, 116
Chocolate Almond Shortbread Bars, 30
Crispy Almond Bars, 28
Frozen Almond Crunch, 100
Frozen Viennese Torte, 102
Mississippi Mud Ice Cream Pie, 95
Peach Almond Pound Cake, 68
Raspberry Almond Bars, 41
Raspberry Almond Tartlets, 65
Triple-Chocolate Cheesecake, 115

Apple
Apple Cake with Caramel Icing, 81
Apple Torte, 116
Buttery Apple Crumble, 112
Double-Crust Apple Pie, 46
Sour Cream Apple Streusel Pie, 44

Apricot
Almond Apricot Shortbread, 27

Banana
Banana Pudding, 110
Banana Split Pie, 97

Blackberry
Blackberry Cobbler, 111
Fresh Fruit Tart, 63

Blueberry
Blueberry Cheesecake Bars, 38
Blueberry Cream Pie, 46
Easy Blueberry Cake, 82
Fresh Fruit Tart, 63

Bourbon
Bourbon Glaze, 108
Bourbon Sauce, 109
Rich Bourbon-Glazed Bread Pudding, 108

Bread Puddings
Butter Pecan Bread Pudding, 109
Rich Bourbon-Glazed Bread Pudding, 108

Brownies
Blonde Brownies, 36
Caramel Pecan Brownies, 32
Chocolate Brownie with Mint Ice Cream, 92
Triple-Layer Chocolate Peanut Butter Brownies, 34
Ultimate Chocolate Brownies, 33

Butterscotch
Butterscotch Sauce, 93
Oatmeal Butterscotch Cookies, 22

Cakes
Angel Food Cake with Strawberries, 82
Apple Cake with Caramel Icing, 81
Caramel Cake, 80
Carrot Cake with Cream Cheese Icing, 84
Chocolate Vegan Death Cake, 75
Easy Blueberry Cake, 82
Gooey Chocolate Crunch Cake, 73
Lemon Layer Cake, 87
Molten Chocolate Cakes with Mint Fudge Sauce, 76
Red Velvet Cake with Cream Cheese Frosting, 78
Refreshing Tropical Fruit Cake, 81
Rich Chocolate Bundt Cake with Chocolate Icing, 74
Sour Cream Coconut Cake, 86
White Chocolate Pecan Cake, 79

Cakes, Pound
Caramel Pound Cake with Caramel Frosting, 70
Chocolate Pound Cake with Chocolate Glaze, 71
Peach Almond Pound Cake, 68
Traditional Pound Cake, 72
White Chocolate Pound Cake, 73

Caramel
Caramel Cake, 80
Caramel Frosting, 32, 70
Caramel Icing, 80, 81
Caramel Pecan Brownies, 32
Caramel Pound Cake with Caramel Frosting, 70
Caramel Sauce, 98, 99, 106
Crème Caramel, 121
Gooey Chocolate Crunch Cake, 73

Cheesecakes
Blueberry Cheesecake Bars, 38
Pecan Pie Cheesecake, 114
Triple-Chocolate Cheesecake, 115

Chocolate. See also Dark Chocolate; White Chocolate
Bittersweet Chocolate Tart, 60
Black Bottom Pie, 54
Chocolate Brownie with Mint Ice Cream, 92
Chocolate Glaze, 71, 115
Chocolate Icing, 74, 119, 123
Chocolate Marshmallow Frosting, 34
Chocolate Pound Cake with Chocolate Glaze, 71
Chocolate Toffee Bars, 37
Chocolate Vegan Death Cake, 75
Creamy Layered Chocolate Dessert, 120
Frozen Viennese Torte, 102
Fudge Nut Gems, 23

Gooey Chocolate Crunch Cake, 73
Molten Chocolate Cakes with Mint Fudge Sauce, 76
Really Chocolate Refrigerator Cookies, 26
Rich Chocolate Bundt Cake with Chocolate Icing, 74
Snowballs, 24
Toffee Chip Ice Cream Squares, 91
Triple-Chocolate Cheesecake, 115
Triple-Layer Chocolate Peanut Butter Brownies, 34
Ultimate Chocolate Brownies, 33

Chocolate Chips
Blonde Brownies, 36
Chocolate Almond Shortbread Bars, 30
Chocolate Toffee Bars, 37
Chocolate Vegan Death Cake, 75
Cookie, 93
Fudge Nut Gems, 23
Giant Ice Cream Sandwich with Butterscotch Sauce, 93
Hot Fudge Sauce, 91, 92, 95, 98
Individual Ice Cream Sandwiches, 94
Mint Hot Fudge Sauce, 76
Rich Chocolate Bundt Cake with Chocolate Icing, 74
Triple Treat Bars, 36
Ultimate Chocolate Brownies, 33
Ultimate Nut and Chocolate Chip Tart, 58

Cobblers
Blackberry Cobbler, 111

Coconut
Sour Cream Coconut Cake, 86
Triple Treat Bars, 36

Coffee
Chocolate Pound Cake with Chocolate Glaze, 71
Chocolate Vegan Death Cake, 75
Espresso Syrup, 124
Frozen Viennese Torte, 102

Jim's Macadamia Nut Tart, 57
Mississippi Mud Ice Cream Pie, 95
Tiramisu, 124
Triple-Layer Chocolate Peanut Butter Brownies, 34
Ultimate Chocolate Brownies, 33

Cookies
Fudge Nut Gems, 23
Giant Ice Cream Sandwich with Butterscotch Sauce, 93
Grandmother Miller's Butter Pecan Crisps, 20
Individual Ice Cream Sandwiches, 94
Macadamia "Butter" Cookies with Dried Cranberries, 19
Oatmeal Butterscotch Cookies, 22
Old-Fashioned Peanut Butter Cookies, 21
Really Chocolate Refrigerator Cookies, 26
Snowballs, 24
Toffee Butter Cookies, 21

Cookies, Bar. *See also* Brownies; Shortbread
Blueberry Cheesecake Bars, 38
Chocolate Toffee Bars, 37
Crispy Almond Bars, 28
Orange Bars with Orange Cream Cheese Frosting, 40
Peanut Butter Bars, 31
Pecan Pie Bars, 41
Raspberry Almond Bars, 41
Triple Treat Bars, 36

Cranberry
Macadamia "Butter" Cookies with Dried Cranberries, 19

Crusts
Almond Crust, 30
Gingersnap Crust, 54
Graham Cracker Crust, 50
Shortbread Crust, 38
Vanilla Wafer Crust, 114

Custard
Crème Caramel, 121
Custard, 110
Custard Filling, 119
Custard Sauce, 112
Microwave Custard, 123

Dark Chocolate
Dark Chocolate Sauce, 100
Dark Chocolate Walnut Pie, 55

Desserts
Boston Cream Pie, 119
Buttery Apple Crumble, 112
Creamy Layered Chocolate Dessert, 120
Custard-Filled Éclairs with Chocolate Icing, 122
Tiramisu, 124

Frostings/Glazes/Icings
Bourbon Glaze, 108
Caramel Frosting, 32, 70
Caramel Icing, 80, 81
Chocolate Icing, 74, 119, 123
Chocolate Glaze, 71, 115
Chocolate Marshmallow Frosting, 34
Cream Cheese Frosting, 78
Cream Cheese Icing, 84
Orange Cream Cheese Frosting, 40
Peanut Butter Frosting, 31
White Chocolate Frosting, 79

Fruit. *See* Apple; Apricot; Banana; Blackberry; Blueberry; Coconut; Cranberry; Lemon; Lime; Orange; Peach; Pineapple; Raisins; Raspberry; Strawberry

Ice Cream
Banana Split Pie, 97
Chocolate Brownie with Mint Ice Cream, 92
Frozen Almond Crunch, 100
Frozen Viennese Torte, 102
Giant Ice Cream Sandwich with Butterscotch Sauce, 93

Individual Ice Cream Sandwiches, 94
Mississippi Mud Ice Cream Pie, 95
Peach Pecan Ice Cream Dessert with Caramel Sauce, 99
Snickers Ice Cream Pie, 98
Toffee Chip Ice Cream Squares, 91

Ice Cream Sandwiches
Giant Ice Cream Sandwich with Butterscotch Sauce, 93
Individual Ice Cream Sandwiches, 94

Lemon
Creamy Lemon White Chocolate Tart, 62
Lemon Curd, 62
Lemon Layer Cake, 87
Lemon-Lime Tart, 63
Lemon Meringue Pie, 47

Lime
Lemon-Lime Tart, 63
Lime Cream Pie in Meringue Shell, 49

Macadamia Nuts
Jim's Macadamia Nut Tart, 57
Macadamia "Butter" Cookies with Dried Cranberries, 19

Meringues
Meringue, 47, 110
Meringue Shell, 49

Mint
Chocolate Brownie with Mint Ice Cream, 92
Mint Hot Fudge Sauce, 76

Nuts. See also Almonds; Macadamia Nuts; Peanuts; Pecans; Pistachios; Walnuts
Toasting, 19
Ultimate Nut and Chocolate Chip Tart, 58

Oats
Buttery Apple Crumble, 112
Oatmeal Butterscotch Cookies, 22
Peanut Butter Bars, 31
Raspberry Almond Bars, 41

Orange
Orange Bars with Orange Cream Cheese Frosting, 40
Orange Cream Cheese Frosting, 40
Refreshing Tropical Fruit Cake, 81

Peach
Peach Almond Pound Cake, 68
Peach Pecan Ice Cream Dessert with Caramel Sauce, 99

Peanut Butter
Old-Fashioned Peanut Butter Cookies, 21
Peanut Butter Bars, 31
Peanut Butter Frosting, 31
Triple-Layer Chocolate Peanut Butter Brownies, 34

Peanuts
Old-Fashioned Peanut Butter Cookies, 21
Snickers Ice Cream Pie, 98

Pecans
Apple Cake with Caramel Icing, 81
Blonde Brownies, 36
Blueberry Cheesecake Bars, 38
Blueberry Cream Pie, 46
Butter Pecan Bread Pudding, 109
Caramel Pecan Brownies, 32
Carrot Cake with Cream Cheese Icing, 84
Chocolate Toffee Bars, 37
Classic Pecan Pie, 53
Fudge Nut Gems, 23
Grandmother Miller's Butter Pecan Crisps, 20
Peach Pecan Ice Cream Dessert with Caramel Sauce, 99
Pecan Pie Bars, 41
Pecan Pie Cheesecake, 114
Pecan Tart, 59
Really Chocolate Refrigerator Cookies, 26
Refreshing Tropical Fruit Cake, 81
Shortbread Crust, 38
Snowballs, 24
Sour Cream Apple Streusel Pie, 44
Streusel Topping, 44
Triple Treat Bars, 36
Ultimate Chocolate Brownies, 33
White Chocolate Pecan Cake, 79

Pies. See also Tarts
Banana Split Pie, 97
Black Bottom Pie, 54
Blueberry Cream Pie, 46
Classic Pecan Pie, 53
Dark Chocolate Walnut Pie, 55
Double-Crust Apple Pie, 46
Fresh Strawberry Pie, 51
Lemon Meringue Pie, 47
Lime Cream Pie in Meringue Shell, 49
Mississippi Mud Ice Cream Pie, 95
Snickers Ice Cream Pie, 98
Sour Cream Apple Streusel Pie, 44
Strawberry Cream Pie, 50
Sweet Potato Pie, 52

Pineapple
Refreshing Tropical Fruit Cake, 81

Pistachios
Jim's Macadamia Nut Tart, 57

Puddings
Banana Pudding, 110
Sticky Toffee Pudding, 106

Raisins
Rich Bourbon-Glazed Bread Pudding, 108

Raspberry
Raspberry Almond Bars, 41
Raspberry Almond Tartlets, 65
Raspberry Linzer Torte, 117

Shortbread
  Almond Apricot Shortbread, 27
  Chocolate Almond Shortbread Bars, 30
  Peach Pecan Ice Cream Dessert with Caramel Sauce, 99
  Shortbread Crust, 38

Strawberry
  Angel Food Cake with Strawberries, 82
  Banana Split Pie, 97
  Fresh Fruit Tart, 63
  Fresh Strawberry Pie, 51
  Strawberry Cream Pie, 50
  Strawberry Topping, 50

Sweet Potatoes
  Sweet Potato Pie, 52

Tarts
  Bittersweet Chocolate Tart, 60
  Creamy Lemon White Chocolate Tart, 62
  Fresh Fruit Tart, 63
  Jim's Macadamia Nut Tart, 57
  Lemon-Lime Tart, 63
  Pecan Tart, 59
  Raspberry Almond Tartlets, 65
  Ultimate Nut and Chocolate Chip Tart, 58

Toffee
  Chocolate Toffee Bars, 37
  Gooey Chocolate Crunch Cake, 73
  Sticky Toffee Pudding, 106
  Toffee Butter Cookies, 21
  Toffee Chip Ice Cream Squares, 91

Toppings. *See also* Frostings/Glazes/Icings
  Amaretto Cinnamon Sauce, 102
  Bourbon Sauce, 109
  Butterscotch Sauce, 93
  Caramel Sauce, 98, 99, 106
  Cheesecake Topping, 38
  Chocolate Topping, 30
  Custard Sauce, 112
  Dark Chocolate Sauce, 100
  Espresso Syrup, 124
  Hot Fudge Sauce, 91, 92, 95, 98
  Mint Hot Fudge Sauce, 76
  Strawberry Topping, 50
  Streusel Topping, 44
  Sweetened Whipped Cream, 121
  Whipped Cream Topping, 54

Tortes
  Apple Torte, 116
  Frozen Viennese Torte, 102
  Raspberry Linzer Torte, 117

Walnuts
  Dark Chocolate Walnut Pie, 55
  Fudge Nut Gems, 23
  Ultimate Chocolate Brownies, 33

White Chocolate
  Creamy Lemon White Chocolate Tart, 62
  Jim's Macadamia Nut Tart, 57
  Triple-Chocolate Cheesecake, 115
  White Chocolate Frosting, 79
  White Chocolate Pecan Cake, 79
  White Chocolate Pound Cake, 73

To order additional copies of

visit www.sweetnessfollows.com